RATIONALISM: THE NATURAL ORDER OF REASON

PRONIL HALDER

I dedicate this book to everyone grappling with doubts about faith and religion, whether you identify as a rationalist, consider yourself religious yet remain open to alternative viewpoints, or are simply curious about different perspectives. If you harbor even a small spark of curiosity about the world and the ideas that shape it, if you are ready to alter your root perspectives if valid reasoning is presented, you embody the essence of rationality. Nurture that seed of inquiry; it deserves the space to grow and flourish. Throughout history, individuals like you have been quietly sought after, as they hold the potential to inspire change and foster understanding.

I also dedicate this book to the memory of Arindam Pal, my dear childhood friend, neighbor, elder brother, and mentor during my formative years. Arindam recently completed his journey in this world, leaving behind a legacy of positivity in a landscape often marred by negativity and betrayal. He imparted to me fundamental lessons in morality that continue to guide me today. Unfortunately, as we grew older, my career took precedence, and we lost touch. I deeply regret not reaching out to him, especially since I was unaware of the struggles he faced with cancer. While I know that dedicating this book cannot change the past or alleviate my feelings of responsibility for not being there, I hope it serves as a tribute to his memory and helps ease some of my pain. Arindam's influence will always be a part of my journey, and I carry his teachings with me as I navigate the complexities of life.

Contents

Contents

Preface

Nature is rational, whether we acknowledge it or not. If you closely observe and deeply contemplate the natural world, you will realize that there is no room for religion or idealism based on physical forces. Instead, the universe adheres strictly to rationality. Rationality is the fundamental principle governing the universe. Although it may appear indifferent, its precision is evident in the emergence of life on Earth. When organic matter transformed into DNA, there was no underlying morality guiding the process. The universe remains indifferent to moral considerations, acting solely on necessity and efficiency. It consistently chooses the most logical and efficient path. This inherent drive to follow the logical path represents rationality. Unlike other idealisms, rationality is not a human invention; it is a principle that nature has ingrained in us.

No matter how much logic and evidence I present, those deeply rooted in faith will be unable to comprehend and grasp the ideas and knowledge presented in this book. The content within these pages requires an analytical mindset, a willingness to question, and the courage to explore beyond pre-existing beliefs. People who hold a faith-based worldview or are comfortable within their existing knowledge, who have no serious desire to expand or alter their understanding, engage in debate, or who are strictly defensive of their current perspectives, people who are faking their curiosity just to estublish and enforce their own ideas, will be wasting their valuable time reading this book.

This book is written for individuals who feel happiness and excitement in critically examining even their most deeply held beliefs and the assumptions they have lived with for ages. It is for those who do not feel stressed when a completely opposing ideology challenges their thinking with compelling reasoning. It is for those ready to re-evaluate themselves, explore new dimensions of thought, and embrace rational inquiry, no matter where it leads. If you are willing to scrutinize even your most fundamental perspectives, then this book will offer you the tools and insights to delve deeper into the natural order of reason.

Before we delve further into this book, unlike introductions in the religious or astrological texts, I strongly recommend that readers approach this material with a completely skeptical mindset. Question every line and be curious. Do not trust this book religiously. Your consciousness is the most precious thing in the universe because it is through it that the world exists. Do not let unquestioned concepts pollute this invaluable entity. Scrutinize every detail, leave no stone unturned, and seek answers to everything. Only if you are fully satisfied should you accept the ideas presented in this book. Do not accept blindly or believe without reason. Instead, analyze, calculate, and decide for yourself whether to accept or deny the contents.

Do not turn rationalism into a belief system. Do not make it another religion.

Birth of Rationalism

CHAPTER I

A Child's Mind

My journey toward rationalism likely began with my deep connection to nature, which I see as the ultimate embodiment of rationality. To truly grasp rationality, certain fundamental traits are essential—curiosity being one of the most crucial. I can vividly recall a time when I was just a child, perhaps 3 or 4 years old, and my aunt gave me a book titled *Eta Ki, Ota Keno*. The title, in Bengali, translates to *What is This? Why is That?* It might seem surprising, but I have a remarkable ability to remember experiences from such a young age.

One of my earliest memories goes back to when I was barely a year old. My mother took me to the beach at Puri. I remember being terrified of the vast sea. But on that day, something clicked within me—I questioned my fear and decided to confront it. Even at that tender age, I felt an instinctive urge to explore the unknown and overcome my fears. Though I've since learned that humans typically don't form memories so early due to underdeveloped brains, this moment is etched clearly in my mind—the sights, the sounds, and even the raw, wordless thoughts I had as a child. In fact, there's a photograph capturing that exact moment.

Returning to the book my aunt gave me—it was the perfect book at the perfect time. I truly think that a book is one of the most powerful forces in the world. It has the potential to alter the trajectory of a person's life, just as this book did for me.

The book was like an encyclopedia for children, filled with more images than text. At that age, I had only just learned to read the alphabet, so the words didn't hold much meaning for me. But the images were enough to ignite a spark of curiosity in my young mind. Though I don't remember many specific details about the book, I know that it planted the first seed of curiosity within me, setting me on the path to discovering the world with a questioning mind.

We didn't have cable TV back then; instead, we relied on a polarized antenna for our television. I'm sure many who grew up in the '90s will remember those long antennas with multiple arms perched on rooftops, just to pick up a couple of government-run channels.

So, even though we had a television, as a kid, my access to entertainment was pretty limited. My main sources of amusement were books and the radio. Fortunately, our house was filled with books—we practically had a mini library. My father and elder sister were both avid readers, and their passion for books meant that our home was always brimming with literature. Most of the collection consisted of Bengali novels and various storybooks, but what really captured my attention were the few encyclopedias we had. They became my gateway to a world of knowledge, sparking my curiosity and shaping my early understanding of the world.

When I was around 7 or 8 years old, I stumbled upon a book that would shape my understanding of the world in profound ways. It was titled "Choto-der Book of Knowledge," meaning "Kids' Book of Knowledge," published by Deb Sahitya Kutir. This wasn't just any book; it was a thick encyclopedia that seemed to encompass the entire universe. From space exploration to quantum physics, mountain expeditions, history, culture, and mythology, it covered everything.

The chapter on space exploration captivated me the most. The tales of discovering new planets, the quests to reach the moon and beyond, the mysteries of interstellar travel, black holes, and wormholes—all of this was like magic to a young mind. It opened my eyes to the vastness of the universe and made me realize that I was part of something much bigger than my immediate surroundings.

This book didn't just fill my mind with wonder; it ignited a desire to understand the world through logic and science. I began to develop a logical approach to life, where everything needed a scientific explanation. I couldn't be satisfied until I found the reasoning behind things—only then could I find peace.

CHAPTER II

A Seed of Doubt

My family followed a typical Hindu lifestyle, much like the other families in our community. There was little that set us apart when it came to religious practices. My parents, especially my father, were devoted worshipers of Lord Jagannath. Ironically, my father was also an active member of the Marxist Communist Party at the time. It wasn't until much later in life that I began to grasp the bitter irony of this contradiction.

Every year, without fail, my father would take us on a pilgrimage to Puri, a sacred city in Odisha, revered as one of Hinduism's holiest sites. It was a place he seemed inexplicably attached to, a comfort zone he refused to step beyond. Despite the world being vast and full of wonders, he resisted any suggestion of visiting other places. As I grew older, I began to question how someone so resistant to change could identify as a communist, a movement often associated with revolutionary ideas and challenging the status quo. Perhaps he never truly understood what it meant to be a communist. Or perhaps, like many others of his time, he simply went along with it without deep reflection.

Growing up, I was expected to be a quiet and obedient follower, though my mind was always brimming with questions—questions that my parents were unable or unwilling to answer. The more they failed to provide explanations, the more my doubts grew. I began to question the very purpose of it all. If God created us, who created God? If He exists, where does He reside? If He lives in the sky, why doesn't He fall down? Does He possess some kind of technology to defy gravity? These questions, born out of my curiosity, slowly started to chip away at the religious teachings I had been raised with, leaving me with a growing sense of uncertainty.

At that time, I lacked the courage and confidence to break free from the rules that society imposed on me. My friends from that period, before I entered high school, were, unfortunately, not very liberal in their thinking. They were wonderful friends, and I still cherish my connections with some of them today. They've been there for me in many difficult situations, and for that, I'm deeply grateful. However, I often felt that they didn't share the same curiosity and doubts that I had. Even now, I observe that much of society operates within this same mindset. Most people are obedient followers, and this obedience to authority provides a sense of reward that perpetuates religious and social norms. I grasped this concept even as a child, though I might not have fully articulated it then. Over time, I began to see a clear division in how people think: those who prioritize logic and reason, and those whose decisions are guided primarily by morality and tradition.

It's often surprising to reflect on how early life began teaching me the lessons of loneliness. I frequently felt that everything around me—my family, friends, society, films, culture, television, and music—stood in opposition to my philosophy. I was a solitary traveler on a path that I came to recognize as rationality.

There was a significant period in my life when I prioritized moral values above all else in my decision-making. It wasn't until a few years ago that I began to truly grasp and embrace the concept of rationalism.

I'll delve into this chapter of my life in detail later in this book. For now, I'm merely highlighting the early sparks of rationalism that were attempting to ignite, albeit sporadically, during my formative years.

CHAPTER III

The Emergence of Conflict

My journey into rationalism began with a leftist mindset, though I've since come to understand that rationalism itself defies conventional political categories. It doesn't fit neatly on the left-right spectrum but rather operates on a higher plane—what I like to think of as the "z-axis" of the political spectrum. This dimension often goes unnoticed, yet it holds the potential to elevate our understanding beyond the binary conflicts of traditional ideologies.

The first conflict I encountered was within myself. As I grappled with my evolving beliefs, this internal struggle soon extended to my family and then to society at large. I realized early on that when I am confident in my convictions, I have no hesitation in defending them. But in contrast, I noticed that religion, at every turn, seemed to be shrouded in hesitation. Religion creates a carefully constructed loop of thought, one that traps individuals and prevents them from breaking free.

Let me explain what I mean. Many religious texts insist that they should be approached with a non-analytical mind. This is crucial because an analytical mind acts as a sharp tool, capable of cutting through dogma. However, religion often counters any questioning by claiming that those who doubt simply haven't embraced its teachings with a truly open, non-analytical mind—a fundamental requirement of the faith. This circular reasoning effectively shuts down logical inquiry, trapping people in a cycle of unquestioning belief.

I know this perspective may anger many, but even the Bhagavad Gita, revered by so many, is not exempt from employing this subtle technique to cultivate unwavering loyalty. If I am confident in my ideas, I welcome challenges; I invite scrutiny. If I have built my beliefs on a foundation of truth and reason, I am not afraid to have others test their strength. I would not resort to trickery to protect them. So, if religious doctrines like those in the Gita or the Quran are as powerful as they claim to be, why do they exhibit fear from the very first page? Why do they discourage the very questioning that could affirm their strength?

These questions fuel my ongoing conflict with the established norms of faith and society, propelling me further down the path of rationalism.

CHAPTER IV

The Foundations of Rationalism

Since I'm not a widely known figure, delving into the depths of my personal biography might not hold much interest. However, I may occasionally need to reference specific life experiences to clarify how or why I arrived at certain conclusions. For now, let's focus on exploring what rationalism truly is and why it is an essential part of human thought.

The pillars of rationalism are straightforward:

1. Analyze everything with logic before reaching a conclusion.
2. Maintain an open mind—be a neutral observer, free from bias.
3. Avoid assumptions and resist being swayed by belief or faith.

These principles aren't human inventions; rather, they are intrinsic to our very nature. Consider the first individual who struck two stones together, creating a spark that led to fire. While others may have idly played with stones, this person became curious about the spark and used analytical thinking to sustain the fire. What else could you call this if not rationalism?

Even the most devoutly faith-driven person cannot be entirely irrational. People often cite the example of someone drowning, crying out to God for help. But have you noticed how the body instinctively flails its arms, trying every possible movement to exploit the buoyancy of water? This reflex is the body's way of logically searching for a way to stay afloat. Isn't that a form of rationalism? The body, even in desperation, is still seeking the most logical solution to survive.

Rationalism, then, is not an abstract concept imposed upon us but a fundamental aspect of human existence. It is the driving force behind our survival, our progress, and our understanding of the world. Without it, we would still be playing with stones, unaware of the fire within our grasp.

I myself though have never called out for God yet even at the few closest encounters of death. I have made myself like this from childhood. I know it is not very easy to do it when we are constantly getting exposed to our religious Indian culture from the very beginning of our life.

This is where my anger and frustration stem from. In our culture, religion is imposed from the very beginning of life, at a time when a person hasn't yet developed a conscious, logical mindset. It's a prime opportunity for religion to take root and grow, unchallenged by reason or critical thought. If this isn't a fear of rationalism, then what is? Why such desperation to embed religion so deeply, so early? It's as if there's an inherent understanding that once a mind is trained to think analytically, the grip of religious dogma might weaken. The urgency to indoctrinate before rational thought can flourish seems like a deliberate effort to suppress questioning, to stifle the natural human impulse to seek truth through logic and reason.

I intentionally emphasized the term 'conscious' because I've come to recognize that rationalism manifests in two distinct forms. The first is what we might call *conscious rationalism*, where we actively engage our logical faculties to make sensible decisions. For instance, if you're faced with the choice between a thick blanket and a thin one on a cold day, you would logically opt for the thicker blanket. This decision is made consciously by evaluating the options and selecting the one that best serves your needs, clearly demonstrating the use of the rational, analytical part of the brain.

The second form is *unconscious rationalism*, which operates at a more instinctual level, beyond our direct control or awareness. This form governs basic reflexes and natural processes that aren't driven by conscious thought but are nonetheless rational in nature. Take, for example, the way your pupils constrict when exposed to bright light. This isn't something you decide to do—it's an automatic response that serves to protect your retinas from potential harm. Although it doesn't involve conscious reasoning, this reflex is still a rational action, as it effectively preserves the integrity of your vision. Over the course of evolution, our bodies have adopted such mechanisms, reflecting a deeply ingrained form of rationalism that ensures our survival.

Faith: Our Enemy

CHAPTER V

The Bias Between Rationalism and Religion

If rationalism is inherently part of our nature, then the question naturally arises: why did religion emerge in the first place? Does it hold any place within the framework of rationalism? If not, why was it created at all?

The truth is that religion, at its inception, was a rational step, but only for a select group of people at the time. To truly understand this, we must examine the origins of religion and the contexts in which they were born.

Religions across the world have vastly different roots, and each was formed for its own unique reasons. Take Hinduism, for example, which, as often claimed, wasn't initially designed as a system for gaining followers or building a unified community. In its earliest forms, it was more of a way of life—a guiding framework for making decisions and navigating complex moral landscapes. We catch a glimpse of this in the Bhagavad Gita, where Lord Krishna offers teachings on life, duty, and ethics. However, even in the Gita, Krishna makes it clear from the outset that the text must be approached with acceptance and an unwavering, doubt-free mind.

Here's an important passage from the Bhagavad Gita, Chapter 7: Shloka 28:

*"tad viddhi praṇipātena parayā bhaktiyogena
sevamānaḥ
śrutvā me saptamyāṁ hy eṣa te yogaḥ praśasyate.*
"

Translation:

"Know that by single-minded devotion you can know Me, and by knowing Me, you will attain to Me. I am the goal of knowledge, the object of meditation, the Supreme Person.
"

This shloka emphasizes the necessity of devotion and surrender to grasp divine wisdom. It suggests that one can only achieve the highest form of knowledge by embracing the teachings without doubt, with absolute faith and dedication. This requirement for unquestioning acceptance of the divine is, in essence, a tool to secure faith and prevent rational inquiry from disrupting belief.

We see a similar pattern in other religious texts. The Quran, for instance, also stresses faith, trust, and submission to God's will. While the Quran may not contain an exact parallel to the Gita's instruction to "read without doubt," it continuously emphasizes faith as a cornerstone of spiritual growth.

Consider these examples from the Quran:

- *Surah Al-Baqarah (2:282): "And those who believe in the Unseen and establish regular prayer, and spend out of what We have provided them, and believe in what was revealed to you and in what was revealed before you, they are the ones who are steadfast on guidance from their Lord."*
- *Surah Al-Baqarah (2:257): "God is the Protector of those who believe. He will lead them out of darkness into light."*

The Quran encourages believers to have unwavering faith in God's plan and submit to His will, reinforcing that only through faith can one attain divine truth. Here again, we see a structure that requires surrendering rational doubt in favor of spiritual certainty.

Similarly, the Bible shares this theme. Though the Bible may not explicitly instruct readers to approach with acceptance and free of doubt, it frequently calls for faith and trust in God's word.

Some relevant biblical passages include:

- *Romans 10:17: "So then faith comes by hearing, and hearing by the word of God." This highlights the importance of accepting and believing in the word of God.*
- *Hebrews 11:1: "Now faith is the assurance of things hoped for, the conviction of things not seen." This verse underscores the essence of faith—belief in what cannot be immediately understood or seen.*

- *John 20:29: "Jesus said to him, 'Because you have seen Me, you have believed. Blessed are those who have not seen and yet have believed.'"*
  This passage praises belief without evidence, emphasizing faith over rational inquiry.

Across these major religions—Hinduism, Islam, and Christianity—the message is consistent: the path to salvation or enlightenment is through unquestioning faith. Each tradition, in its own way, conveys that to achieve the ultimate spiritual goal, one must accept divine teachings without doubt or critical analysis.

What this reveals is that while religion may have originated as a rational framework for a select few, it has evolved into a system that often discourages rational inquiry. At its core, religion seeks to shield itself from the disruptive force of questioning minds. It is this very resistance to doubt and rational examination that draws a clear line between the foundational tenets of religion and those of rationalism. Religion, in many ways, can be seen as a reaction to the fear of rationalism, a way to secure faith by preemptively disallowing questions.

The recurring theme is simple and coherent, regardless of the religion's origin: "Accept me without question, or you will not reach your goal."

Earlier, I mentioned that religion was rational only for a select few. If we look deeper into Hinduism, we often find religious texts written in the context of great kings or rulers. These kings had a vested interest in preserving their legacy and maintaining influence over future generations. To accomplish this, they needed systems that could cement their authority even after their reign. Enter the Rishis—sages who wrote these texts, often infusing them with mysticism and divine narratives to attract followers and cement their own influence. By attributing "divine" powers to themselves, they ensured their position in society. The Brahmins, who were responsible for performing rituals, added layers of complexity and fear into religious practices, ensuring that the masses remained dependent on them for spiritual guidance. Why? Because hard work or rational thinking might not be attractive to everyone. Fear, especially the fear of God, is a much more compelling and easily exploitable tool.

The most profound effect of religion, however, is on its followers. Religion doesn't change minds in an overt or immediate way; it works slowly and subtly, embedding itself so deeply into the fabric of thought that even highly educated people often fail to question it—or worse, they actively resist any attempt to break free from its influence.

A religious follower is typically bound by rules that they rarely question. In return, they receive a false sense of security—the belief that a higher power is looking out for them. They keep giving, sacrificing their time, money, and energy, because every religion teaches its followers to maintain faith indefinitely. This idea of eternal faith is one of the most powerful and insidious aspects of religion.

Now, let's consider the Brahmin's role. For him, religion is a rational strategy. It guarantees his survival and provides a way to make a living. His livelihood depends on the rituals and beliefs he maintains for the community. For the Brahmin, continuing the system is a logical choice.

But what about the person who earns ₹8000 a month, barely enough to meet his family's basic needs? Is it rational for him to spend money every week on offerings, incense sticks, flowers, and elaborate religious ceremonies, knowing it leaves little for his children's education or well-being? This person is trapped in the cycle of religious devotion, but in truth, it's a system that offers him nothing tangible in return—just an endless promise of divine favor that never arrives.

It's crucial to understand that religion itself is not the root enemy of rationalism—it is merely a byproduct. The real source is faith. Faith is the seed from which religion grows. Faith, in its essence, is the absence of an analytical mind. It is what people turn to when their minds are tired or overwhelmed. Just as the body needs rest, so too does the mind, and faith offers an easy respite. However, faith is a temporary relief, not a solution. It replaces the hard work of thinking and reasoning with blind trust.

People also gravitate toward faith because it promises something for nothing. The idea of receiving rewards without hard work is deeply appealing, and religion provides this false hope. For example, in my religion, like many others, the Sun is worshipped as a god. People believe that to get closer to the Sun—this divine entity—they must offer prayers and perform rituals. But have they ever stopped to consider that to truly know something, you must study it, observe it, understand its nature? To genuinely get closer to the Sun, one should study its properties, observe its behavior, and calculate its movements. That is how you come to know the Sun—through knowledge, not worship.

But when you present this to people, they often reject it. Why? Because deep down, they know that this path requires effort, and effort is not what they want. Religion offers them a way out—an assurance that simply by performing rituals and prayers, they can achieve what they seek. However, the truth is that they never really wanted to get closer to the Sun, not in any meaningful way. If they did, they would acknowledge that it requires hard work, and sometimes, that hard work does not align with the comfortable image they have in mind.

In the end, people choose the easier path, the path of faith, because they know that true understanding, true knowledge, requires effort. And sometimes, that effort doesn't look the way they expect or desire it to.

CHAPTER VI

Other Byproducts of Faith

Religion is not the only byproduct of faith. In fact, there are many others: superstition, astrology, homeopathy, belief in the afterlife, voodoo, and similar practices all stem from the same source—faith. These subjects exist in a realm where logical questioning is either discouraged or outright ignored. People seem unwilling to engage their analytical thought process when dealing with these matters, preferring the simplicity and comfort that faith provides. Faith convinces them that there is something beyond reason, something they must simply accept without challenge.

Think about it: if a stranger on the street offered you food, claiming it would improve your health, would you accept it without questioning? Of course not! You would naturally be skeptical and protective of yourself. So why is it that when we are at our most vulnerable, when our lives demand careful consideration and strategy, we so readily surrender to faith? We abandon our defenses and accept beliefs without a second thought, often at the exact moment we need rationality the most.

It is not a coincidence that all these byproducts of faith—superstition, astrology, homeopathy, and so on—fall under the same umbrella as religion. They all share the same root: the suspension of critical thinking. When a person embraces one of these beliefs, it becomes much easier for them to accept others. This mindset slowly but surely guides them down an uncertain and self-destructive path. And because society is made up of individuals, this collective abandonment of reason leads to the deterioration of the society as a whole.

Consider a household where parents regularly offer prayers and rituals to lifeless statues, teaching their children that these actions have real power. The children observe, absorb, and eventually internalize this behavior. They develop the mindset of unquestioning faith, believing that this is the way the world works. At some point, they will apply this mindset to other areas of their lives, making decisions based not on reason or logic, but on blind faith. Over time, a society of unquestioning individuals will emerge, a society that chooses not to ask "why" or "how," but simply accepts things as they are told.

This societal shift toward unquestioning belief can have profound consequences, and in the next chapter, we will explore the long-term fate of such a society. What happens when a culture abandons critical thinking and analytical reasoning in favor of faith? What does that mean for progress, for innovation, for humanity's future? These are the questions we will confront next.

CHAPTER VII

A Happy Society Does Not Mean a Healthy Society

One of the most clever deceptions of faith is its ability to convince people that everything is fine, even when nothing is fine in reality.

Ask yourself: have you ever noticed a group of people who blindly follow a person or ideology without any logical questioning and try to establish whatever path that person gave them? History offers countless examples, and we see it in the present as well. It's not limited to religion. Think about Hitler and his millions of followers, or even the political parties of today—both left and right. Their supporters don't often build their worldview on rationalism. Instead, their thoughts, actions, and outcomes revolve around a person, or a man-made ideology.

The truth is simple: any ideology created by humans will be imperfect. Whether it's communism, socialism, democracy, or any other philosophy—or religious texts like the Bhagavad Gita, the Quran, or the Bible—none are without flaws. Even if a creator existed, why would they write ideologies on paper? Wouldn't it be more logical to engrain those principles in our very being? If there were a divine plan, why would it need to be recorded in books of shlokas and verses?

The ideology ingrained within us, however, is rationalism—the only ideology that nature gave us biologically, not written in any book. Rationalism exists in our capacity to think logically, to question, to understand the world around us through observation and reasoning.

We live in the third dimension, but there are many other dimensions existing alongside us. The third dimension is basic—it has a starting and ending point for nearly everything. This is why humans tend to seek origins for everything and why people have a compulsion to establish the existence of creators—whether it's God, Allah, or Jesus—as the "starting point" for the universe. But the universe is far more complex than our three-dimensional brains can fully comprehend. In reality, the universe doesn't need a starting point as we conceive it; it originates and terminates within itself. Our minds may struggle to imagine this, but it can be understood mathematically.

The universe itself is a perfect example of how complexity can flourish from nothing. It operates with pure, unbiased rationalism, following natural laws without the need for a divine creator. If we aspire to understand the universe, we too must follow the path of rationalism.

Now, back to the original question: how does faith affect an entire society when people shift toward it on an individual level? Initially, it may seem like there's no significant impact. But faith is like a disease—capable of spreading in subtle yet pervasive ways. A person's faith-based actions and philosophy are observed and absorbed by those around them. From the individual to the family, and eventually to the society, this mindset spreads.

Once a society is infected by this faith-driven mindset, it creates opportunities for exploitation. A mind incapable of logical thinking is easy prey. Politicians, religious leaders, and astrologers have long understood this. That's why we have so many theocratic nations, religious political parties, and extreme ideological organizations—backed by millions who do not center rationalism in their thinking. Even when their leaders promote irrational ideas, followers rush to defend them, as if their own identity or reputation is at stake. Faith, acting as a self-protective mechanism, drives this behavior.

This phenomenon is similar to how rabies operates. The rabies virus infects the nervous system and spreads through saliva. A rabies patient can't drink water because the virus "instructs" the brain to fear water, ensuring the saliva isn't washed away and the virus can continue to spread. In much the same way, faith invades the mind, triggering defensiveness whenever logic is introduced. Even when a person infected by faith knows that rationalism offers the truth, they resist it. Faith, like the rabies virus, "knows" that rationalism is the antidote—and it will do whatever it can to prevent its host from being cured.

In this way, faith ensures its own survival, even at the expense of the individual's and society's wellbeing. A happy society is not necessarily a healthy one, and as faith spreads, the very health of rational thought—the foundation of progress—begins to deteriorate.

CHAPTER VIII

Faith vs. Trust

When discussing faith, people often mistakenly conflate it with trust, but the two are fundamentally different. Faith involves accepting a conclusion without any form of analytical reasoning or evidence, while trust is a projection based on past experiences and reliable data points.

Let's break this down. Faith is the act of accepting something without scrutiny, without examining the evidence, or without considering alternative possibilities. In contrast, trust is built over time, grounded in experiences that consistently support the reliability of a person, idea, or system. Trust requires a pattern of evidence, a history of proven outcomes that allows one to make a rational decision based on prior knowledge.

Here's an example: many people place faith in the existence of a god. However, there is no verifiable or inevitable proof of that god's existence. In this case, no one has any solid past data points to support the belief. Moreover, believers often avoid engaging in critical examination of this belief, preferring not to question it. Hence, two critical checkmarks are missed:

1. Was the conclusion driven by valid past data points?
2. Was an analytical thought process involved in reaching the conclusion?

In the case of faith in a god, neither criterion is fulfilled. Therefore, this belief system is based on faith.

Now, consider another example. Suppose a close friend asks to borrow money. You know this person well: they have helped you in the past, they have always kept their word, and they have proven themselves trustworthy on multiple occasions. When you decide to lend them money, two things happen:

1. **Was the conclusion driven by valid past data points?** – Yes, the friend's past behavior (loyalty, honesty, and reliability) gives you a foundation to base your decision on.
2. **Was an analytical thought process executed?** – Yes, you logically evaluate the friend's past actions and predict their future behavior, trusting that they will repay the money.

This is trust—an informed, rational conclusion derived from past experiences and analytical thought.

Faith, on the other hand, bypasses this process entirely. You cannot "trust" a god or supernatural entity in the same way you trust a friend because there are no valid past data points or rational projections involved. Faith, by definition, is accepting something without evidence or logical evaluation.

Trust is beneficial to society, promoting strong relationships and fostering positive social interactions. It is a tool for collaboration, understanding, and community-building. You can trust family members, friends, colleagues, and employees based on shared experiences and observable behavior, contributing to healthier relationships and more productive societies.

However, the boundary between faith and trust is often blurred, and this misunderstanding is frequently exploited.

Religious leaders and conservative ideologies often conflate the two, encouraging people to place faith in things without questioning them, by disguising faith as trust. This manipulation helps sustain the stronghold of religion or dogma, stifling critical thinking and allowing those in power to maintain control over the masses.

Recognizing and maintaining this distinction between faith and trust is essential for navigating life with clarity. It allows you to evaluate situations and relationships based on evidence and logic, not blind belief, ensuring that your decisions are grounded in reality rather than unexamined assumptions.

Now that we've established the difference between faith and trust, it's clear how this distinction has been cleverly exploited in religious texts. These texts often urge followers to "trust" in god, but upon closer examination, what they are really advocating for is faith—acceptance without questioning or evidence. They blur the lines deliberately, using the word "trust" to make their message seem rational and justified, when in fact, it bypasses the critical, analytical process we associate with trust.

Religious teachings often emphasize trust in a higher power, but they do so without offering any verifiable evidence or past experiences to support such trust. This is the hallmark of faith, not trust. The teachings rely on the assumption that followers will not question this substitution of terms, reinforcing a mindset where belief without evidence is equated with the reasoned conclusions we arrive at through trust.

This fine manipulation helps sustain the power of religious ideologies. By framing faith as trust, they create an illusion of reliability and credibility, asking followers to believe not based on evidence or experience but on blind acceptance. This exploitation keeps people within the framework of faith, as they are misled into thinking that their beliefs are grounded in something more substantial than mere acceptance.

In essence, religious texts advocate for faith but disguise it as trust, knowing that trust is a concept we value because it is based on real-world experiences and logical thinking. By conflating the two, they make faith seem more reasonable and acceptable, preventing followers from questioning the underlying lack of evidence.

Break the Cycle

CHAPTER IX

The Science of Reaching Conclusions

We live in an age dominated by technology and information. Education and access to knowledge have become so widespread that it's hard to imagine someone being completely irrational. However, despite this easy access to facts and science, we still see a curious blend of rational and irrational thinking in society. Religious and conservative influences often result in people balancing a mixture of logical thought and superstition.

Take a look around, and you'll see that even well-educated people hold onto beliefs in things like superstition, astrology, and black magic. Despite their exposure to the workings of the natural world, they construct mental boundaries where logic no longer applies. The education and scientific principles they learned seem to stop short when confronted with their deeply ingrained irrational beliefs.

I've witnessed this firsthand, even among my closest friends. We all received similar educations. We learned about the laws of physics, the universe, and the natural order of things, yet somehow, these lessons never truly took root in some of them. It's as if the essence of what we were taught never sank in.

Recently, one of my female friends shared a personal experience regarding astrology. She explained how she had applied astrological calculations and that they seemed to work for her. She said she followed the steps in astrological books, input the data, and the outcomes aligned with her life experiences.

Intrigued, I asked her about the type of calculations she used. She explained that she placed values in an astrological chart and followed the prescribed steps.

Then I asked, "How did you conclude that these steps were logical or scientifically valid?"

Her response was that the outcomes matched her life experiences, so she accepted them as true.

This is where the flaw becomes evident. She didn't question the legitimacy of the calculations or seek to understand how they were derived. She simply focused on the fact that the outcome seemed to align with her life. In other words, she skipped over the crucial step of verifying whether the process was grounded in rationality, and instead accepted the outcome at face value.

However, this approach to drawing conclusions is fundamentally flawed. The fact that the result appeared correct does not mean the underlying process was sound. There could be a range of factors—completely unrelated to astrology—that produced the outcome. What undeniable proof can be offered that would make these calculations immune to questioning? The answer is none.

It's important to remember that conclusions should only be made when all possibilities are accounted for and every question has been addressed. When we form a conclusion based on incomplete information or insufficient analysis, we're not drawing a conclusion at all—we're making an assumption.

In my view, assumption-based thinking is one of the most dangerous mindsets of this century. People make critical, often irreversible, mistakes because they fail to differentiate between assumptions and facts. My friend, in this case, assumed the astrological calculations were valid because they produced a favorable result. But she didn't evaluate the origin of the methods, nor did she analyze how the calculations were derived. She simply accepted them because someone else had researched them (an assumption in itself), and because they worked for her once, she considered them true.

This highlights a glaring gap in education. People fall into irrational traps daily because they don't fully understand how to distinguish between assumption and fact. They lack the critical thinking skills to evaluate the evidence before them. This gap in knowledge paves the way for people to be drawn deeper into superstition and irrational beliefs.

Faith, as we discussed earlier, compounds this problem by acting as a self-preservation mechanism, reinforcing these irrational beliefs. When combined with the lack of critical thinking, it forms a formidable trap that is difficult to escape unless one experiences a moment of self-realization. Like any philosophy, the enlightenment of rationality must come from within. Others can guide, but ultimately, it's the individual's choice to accept or reject the "medicine."

In conclusion, never base your beliefs on assumptions, circumstantial evidence, incomplete research, or insufficient data. Doing so will lead to misunderstandings, and once these false conclusions are internalized, they will be accepted as facts. This paves the way for further confusion and darkness. The only way out of this cycle is to rigorously question every piece of information, ensuring it holds up to scrutiny before accepting it as truth.

CHAPTER X

The Pareidolia Effect

In the example discussed in the previous chapter, we encounter a psychological phenomenon that significantly influenced the girl's decision-making process: the Pareidolia effect.

Pareidolia refers to the human tendency to perceive recognizable patterns, shapes, or objects in random, unrelated stimuli. It's why we often see familiar images in clouds, rocks, or even random splashes of paint. For instance, people might spot a rabbit in a cloud or a face on the surface of the moon. This phenomenon occurs because our brains are wired to seek patterns in the world around us, a survival mechanism that helps us make sense of our surroundings. Even when no real pattern exists, we instinctively try to find meaning in chaos.

To put it simply, Pareidolia is the human tendency to link unrelated or irrational stimuli to something familiar or meaningful. While this ability to recognize patterns has been essential for human survival, helping us avoid danger and make quick decisions, it can also strengthen irrational beliefs when applied inappropriately.

The girl's belief in astrology is a prime example of Pareidolia at play. She linked the vague and ambiguous outcomes of astrological predictions to specific experiences in her life. Astrological readings rarely offer concrete details; instead, they provide broad, generalized predictions that are open to interpretation. This creates an incomplete or "blurry" image, and as humans, we naturally try to connect the dots to form a coherent picture. In the case of astrology, the girl made the mistake of overlaying her personal experiences onto these blurry outcomes, perceiving them as a perfect match.

This is the core of how Pareidolia operates. It tricks us into creating connections where none exist. While it's a useful cognitive tool in some situations, it can lead us astray when applied to things like superstitions, pseudosciences, or irrational beliefs. Astrological predictions, much like the clouds we stare at in the sky, are vague enough that anyone can project their own experiences onto them, making it seem like they are eerily accurate.

Understanding the Pareidolia effect is crucial if we want to prevent ourselves from falling into the trap of drawing conclusions based on false connections. It's important to recognize when we are being led by this phenomenon so that our decisions and beliefs remain grounded in reason and evidence. By being aware of when we are connecting dots that aren't really there, we can ensure that our conclusions remain unbiased, logical, and organic.

In the end, the Pareidolia effect is a reminder of how easily the human mind can be swayed by its natural tendencies. While our pattern-seeking abilities are a testament to the incredible complexity of our brains, they also underscore the importance of critical thinking. We must constantly question whether the patterns we see are real or simply the result of our brain's instinctual need to make sense of randomness.

CHAPTER XI

The Placebo and Nocebo Effect

In the world of psychology and human behavior, two fascinating phenomena illustrate how deeply our minds influence our bodies, decisions, and perceptions of reality: the placebo effect and its lesser-known counterpart, the nocebo effect. These concepts highlight how our beliefs, expectations, and mindset can shape not only our physical health but also our reactions to the world around us—sometimes with positive outcomes, and other times with harmful consequences.

- The Placebo Effect

The placebo effect occurs when an individual experiences genuine improvement in their symptoms or overall health after receiving a treatment that, in itself, has no therapeutic value. This could be something as simple as a sugar pill, a saline injection, or even a fake surgery. The critical factor is the person's belief that the treatment is real and effective. This belief alone triggers a positive response in the body, demonstrating the immense power of the mind in shaping physical outcomes.

For example, consider a clinical trial for a new pain medication. Some participants receive the actual drug, while others unknowingly take a placebo—such as a sugar pill. Interestingly, many of those who take the placebo report a significant reduction in pain, even though the pill contains no active ingredients. Their belief that they are receiving real medicine triggers a response in the brain that releases natural painkillers like endorphins, leading to a real alleviation of pain.

This effect reveals the complex relationship between perception and reality. The mere expectation of healing, rather than any medicinal property, can result in measurable improvement. The placebo effect thus demonstrates how much influence our mental state has on our physical well-being.

- The Nocebo Effect

On the other hand, the nocebo effect works in the opposite direction, highlighting how negative expectations or beliefs can lead to worse outcomes. In this case, people experience adverse symptoms or reactions simply because they expect something bad to happen, even if they have not been exposed to any harmful substance or factor.

For example, if a patient is informed that a medication might cause severe side effects, they may start to experience those symptoms—such as nausea, dizziness, or headaches—even if they were only given a placebo. Their belief that something harmful is occurring triggers real physiological responses, underscoring how deeply the mind influences the body.

The nocebo effect is not limited to the medical field. It can also be observed in everyday situations. For instance, if someone is convinced that eating a particular food will make them sick, they may actually feel ill after consuming it, regardless of the food's actual content. This effect highlights how negative beliefs and expectations can create a self-fulfilling prophecy, where the mind's fear or anxiety leads to real, physical discomfort.

Both the placebo and nocebo effects serve as powerful reminders of the profound connection between our minds and bodies. They demonstrate how our perceptions, beliefs, and expectations can shape not only our health but also our decisions and understanding of the world. These effects can be seen in a wide range of human experiences, extending far beyond medical treatments.

The placebo effect is not just a medical phenomenon; it plays a critical role in reinforcing religious beliefs, superstitions, and other irrational practices. Consider the example from the previous chapter of the girl who trusted in astrological predictions. Once she saw some of her life events aligning with astrological forecasts, her belief in the system was strengthened, even though these outcomes may have been coincidences or vague enough to apply to many situations. She fell into the trap of the placebo effect, where her belief in the supernatural made her perceive astrological predictions as effective and accurate.

Even when future astrological predictions don't match her experiences or are filled with gaps and inconsistencies, the placebo effect still influences her thinking. She continues to believe in astrology because her mind has been conditioned to expect positive outcomes, reinforcing the belief that supernatural powers are working in her favor. This is how deeply the placebo effect can penetrate human psychology, making it difficult for individuals to question or abandon their beliefs even when confronted with contrary evidence.

Similarly, the nocebo effect plays a role in the reinforcement of fear-based beliefs and superstitions. When individuals believe that certain actions, objects, or events will bring bad luck or harm, they often begin to experience anxiety, stress, or even physical symptoms in anticipation of the perceived negative outcome. For example, if someone believes that walking under a ladder will bring misfortune, they may feel anxious or experience minor mishaps afterward, attributing these events to their earlier "bad luck" rather than mere coincidence.

This fear-driven nocebo effect can perpetuate irrational thinking, making it difficult for individuals to break free from superstitious beliefs or negative expectations. Over time, these beliefs can become deeply ingrained, influencing not only their emotional state but also their physical well-being.

Both the placebo and nocebo effects demonstrate the extraordinary power of the human mind in shaping our experiences. The placebo effect shows us how positive beliefs and expectations can lead to real improvements in our health and well-being, while the nocebo effect warns us of the dangers of negative thinking and fear. Understanding these effects allows us to recognize the profound influence that our beliefs—rational or otherwise—have on our lives, and how they can either heal or harm us.

In a broader sense, these phenomena also reveal how easily we can be led to embrace irrational beliefs or practices when they seem to produce real outcomes. Recognizing when we are under the influence of such psychological effects is key to cultivating a more rational, evidence-based approach to our decisions and understanding of the world. By doing so, we can avoid falling into the traps of superstition, fear, and unfounded beliefs, and instead seek knowledge and truth based on sound reasoning and complete evidence.

CHAPTER XII

The Rosenthal Effect

The Rosenthal effect, also known as the Pygmalion effect, is a psychological phenomenon where the expectations placed on individuals significantly impact their performance. High expectations often lead to improved performance, while low expectations can result in poorer outcomes. This concept is a powerful reminder of how our perceptions and beliefs about others can shape their actions and potential, creating a self-fulfilling prophecy. When someone expects something to happen, their behavior may unintentionally cause that expectation to come true. The belief itself, whether positive or negative, can influence reality through subtle changes in behavior. When people have high expectations placed upon them, they are often treated more favorably—receiving greater attention, encouragement, and opportunities. This positive treatment fosters increased confidence, motivation, and, ultimately, better performance. Conversely, when low expectations are placed on individuals, they may receive less attention and support. This lack of reinforcement can diminish their confidence and motivation, leading to poorer performance, even if they are capable of more. A teacher might tell a group of students that they are "gifted" and expected to excel in a math competition. These students, believing in their teacher's high expectations, may work harder and put more effort into preparation. As a result, their performance surpasses what might have been expected in a neutral setting. In this case, the teacher's high expectations became a driving force for the students' success.

Our cultural environment is often saturated with religious beliefs that suggest a higher power—be it a god or a spiritual force—is always watching, judging, and guiding our lives. From an early age, many of us observe our parents and elders making sacrifices, offering prayers, and devoting their lives to an unseen creator. These practices expose us to the idea that this divine presence holds significant influence over our actions and outcomes.

Due to this consistent exposure, we may develop high expectations of divine intervention in our lives. For instance, in moments of crisis or challenge, many people call upon God for help, believing that divine assistance will empower them. In certain situations, this belief may indeed improve their physical or mental performance—an example of the Rosenthal effect in play. Their expectation of help from a higher power boosts their confidence, leading to enhanced results in the short term.

However, over time, constantly attributing one's successes and failures to an unseen force can distort an individual's psychological well-being. Continually relying on an external, nonexistent entity to drive one's actions can erode self-reliance and create mental strain. This mental strain can manifest in various forms, including mental disorders such as:

- **Split personality disorder:** When people mentally divide their own identity, sometimes attributing actions to divine or supernatural forces.
- **Schizophrenia:** A condition in which individuals experience delusions and hallucinations, sometimes believing that inanimate objects are alive or that they are possessed by spirits.

- **Animism:** The belief that lifeless objects possess living qualities. While common in young children, this belief, when carried into adulthood, can indicate a deeper mental health issue.

Even in modern times, some societies misinterpret these disorders as ghost possession or spiritual phenomena, failing to recognize the psychological basis behind them.

Let's consider a scenario to understand how the Rosenthal effect, when applied through the lens of religious conservatism, can contribute to the development of mental disorders at an individual and societal level.

Imagine a young boy who, from childhood, watches his parents regularly praying to statues, believing that these lifeless objects contain a divine presence. The child absorbs this idea, and as he grows up, it solidifies into a belief that statues and other inanimate objects might possess consciousness. Though science tells us that matter is lifeless, his mind, influenced by early conditioning, begins to reject this notion. This belief can gradually extend to other areas of his life, leading to a form of Animism—where inanimate objects are perceived to be alive.

This belief, while seemingly harmless, can develop into more serious mental health conditions such as Schizophrenia, individuals might experience hallucinations or delusions about inanimate objects being sentient or delusiinal disorder, where people hold fixed, irrational beliefs about objects or events, despite evidence to the contrary.

Moreover, in societies with a strong focus on religious practices, overexposure to these beliefs can lead to an environment where psychological disorders go unnoticed or are misinterpreted. People might dismiss symptoms of mental illness as spiritual experiences, preventing individuals from seeking the help they need.

It is crucial to understand the implications of the Rosenthal effect, especially when linked to religious or superstitious beliefs. While high expectations can enhance performance in the short term, relying on supernatural forces or external entities for validation can lead to psychological harm. Left unchecked, this can not only affect individuals but also spread through communities, shaping societal norms and attitudes toward mental health.

To foster a healthy society, it is vital to identify, understand, and protect ourselves from the negative consequences of irrational beliefs. Recognizing the role that expectations—whether from religion, superstition, or pseudoscience—play in shaping mental health is the first step toward promoting a more rational and evidence-based understanding of the world. By doing so, we can build a society that values critical thinking and mental well-being, ensuring healthier and more fulfilling lives for future generations.

CHAPTER XIII

Manipulation Techniques

Religion, pseudoscience, astrology, and superstitions often utilize psychological manipulation techniques to influence the behavior and beliefs of individuals and large groups. By employing tactics that tap into emotional, social, and cognitive biases, these belief systems can reinforce adherence, loyalty, and conformity.

- Foot-in-the-Door Technique:

This technique involves getting people to agree to small, seemingly harmless commitments before escalating the demands. In religion and superstitions:

People may first be asked to participate in small rituals, such as lighting candles or attending occasional services. Over time, these small actions can escalate into larger commitments, such as regular tithing, pilgrimages, or more intense spiritual obligations. Astrological readings may start with vague, general advice ("You might meet someone interesting this week") and gradually increase to more specific, life-altering decisions ("You should move to another city or marry this person based on your horoscope").

- Door-in-the-Face Technique:

Here, a large, unreasonable request is made initially, only to be followed by a smaller one that seems more acceptable by comparison.

Religions might initially present extreme or life-altering demands (such as complete renunciation of material possessions), which followers are unlikely to agree to. After rejecting these, they may more readily accept less radical, yet still significant, sacrifices (such as regular donations or fasting). Someone may first be told that not following a particular superstition will result in grave misfortune (e.g., breaking a mirror causing 7 years of bad luck). When they reject this, a milder action, like knocking on wood to prevent bad luck, becomes more acceptable.

- Scarcity Principle:

This principle plays on the idea of limited availability or time, creating urgency and fear of missing out. Many religions emphasize limited opportunities for salvation or enlightenment. Phrases like "This is your only chance for salvation" or "End times are near" encourage urgency in people's adherence to religious rules. Astrological predictions and superstitions often stress that certain events or periods are rare and highly significant (e.g., "The planetary alignment will only happen once in your lifetime," "This ritual must be performed at a precise time to work"), pushing people to act quickly to avoid missing out.

- Authority Principle:

Appealing to figures of authority (whether real or perceived) can add weight to a belief or practice. Religious leaders, texts, or gods are often cited as ultimate authorities. The authority of scriptures or religious leaders is rarely questioned, leading people to accept teachings without critical thought. Pseudoscience often presents "experts" or credentialed individuals who support unverified claims. Similarly, astrology appeals to the authority of ancient wisdom, claiming that celestial knowledge has been passed down by sages, even when lacking scientific validation.

- Liking Principle:

People are more likely to be persuaded by someone they like or feel a connection to. Charismatic religious leaders or preachers often build rapport with their congregations through kindness, compassion, and personal attention. The more followers feel connected to these leaders, the more they trust their guidance. In communities where superstitions are widely followed, people may adopt these practices because they see others they like or respect engaging in them, making the practices seem more credible or necessary.

- Social Proof:

This technique leverages the idea that if many people are doing something, it must be the right thing to do. Organized religions often use the behavior of the majority to enforce conformity. Attending large religious gatherings, witnessing others' devotion, or seeing widespread participation in rituals creates a sense of collective agreement and encourages individuals to follow suit. When people see friends, family, or celebrities following astrology or other pseudoscientific practices, they are more likely to believe in its legitimacy. Social proof reinforces the idea that "everyone else believes it, so it must be true."

- Commitment and Consistency Principle:

People have a psychological desire to appear consistent with their previous commitments. Once they have made a small commitment, they are more likely to continue in that direction to avoid cognitive dissonance. People who have made small commitments to religious practices (such as attending services) feel pressure to remain consistent with their beliefs, leading to larger commitments (e.g., baptisms, conversions, or public declarations of faith). The more invested they become, the harder it is to break away without feeling inconsistent. Once someone consults an astrologer or adheres to a pseudoscientific belief, they may feel compelled to follow subsequent predictions or treatments to remain consistent with their initial commitment.

- Reciprocity Principle:

When someone gives us something, we feel obligated to give something in return. This principle is often exploited to create a sense of indebtedness. Religious institutions may offer comfort, community, or promises of salvation in exchange for loyalty, devotion, or financial contributions. By offering spiritual guidance or "blessings," followers feel compelled to give back through donations or acts of faith. Astrologers and fortune-tellers often offer initial free readings or advice, making people feel obliged to pay for further services or heed their guidance in the future.

These manipulation techniques are often intertwined and applied subtly, causing people to internalize irrational beliefs over time. Once embedded, such beliefs become resistant to critical thinking, leading individuals and even societies to make decisions based on superstition, pseudoscience, or religious dogma rather than reason or evidence.

In the case of religion and superstitions, entire cultural norms and values may evolve around these manipulations. The result is a widespread adoption of irrational behaviors and resistance to scientific or logical explanations. This hinders intellectual growth and promotes a culture where questioning authority or established practices is discouraged.

Understanding how these techniques manipulate belief systems allows individuals to recognize and resist such influences, fostering critical thinking and rationality over emotional manipulation.

Fabric of Reality

CHAPTER XIV

Polymaric Chain of Events

In the universe, all changes and events stem from actions—whether driven by human choices, natural forces, or the influence of external entities. This sequence of actions forms what can be thought of as a polymaric chain of events. Each event is like a monomer, a basic unit in a larger sequence, contributing to a more complex and interconnected outcome.

When analyzing any event, you can divide it into smaller, sequential components or monomers. Each monomer is the smallest possible change or action within an event. For example, consider a car accident involving a pedestrian. This single incident can be broken down into a series of smaller events:

1. **The pedestrian crosses the road:** This decision may stem from the pedestrian's mental state or actions leading up to the moment, perhaps distracted by a previous interaction.
2. **The car approaches:** The driver's actions, like speeding or failing to notice the pedestrian, add to the sequence.
3. **The collision occurs:** The physical impact is the final stage in this chain of events.

By examining these individual components or monomers, we gain a deeper understanding of how the event unfolded and the roles of various actions.

Each event can be conceptualized as having three main parts:

- **Initial Phase (A):** The starting state or condition before any action occurs.
- **Ending Phase (B):** The resulting state after the action has taken place.
- **Initiator or Influencer (C):** The driving force or entity that causes the transition from state A to state B.

For an event to move from A to B, an initiator (C) must act as a catalyst, driving the process forward. The resulting state B then becomes the initial state for the next event, and this sequence continues, creating a chain.

This chain of events is akin to a polymer in chemistry. In a polymer, long chains of monomers connect to form complex structures. Similarly, in an event chain, each individual monomer (or event) connects to the next, building a sequence that culminates in larger, interconnected incidents. The repetition and connection between these unit events form what we can call a polymaric chain of events.

Understanding events as polymaric chains reveals the intricate web of causes and effects that shape our experiences. It emphasizes that every action has a series of underlying components. By dissecting events into monomers, we can better comprehend how individual actions contribute to larger outcomes. This concept can be applied to understand personal choices, historical events, societal trends, or even natural phenomena, revealing the complex and interdependent nature of the world.

In recognizing these chains, we gain insights into how our choices can lead to specific consequences, empowering us to make more informed decisions. This approach also encourages a broader perspective, highlighting that seemingly isolated events often form part of a much larger, interconnected chain.

This theory is entirely born from my personal observations and reflections, and I know there must be room for refinement. I welcome discussions and differing viewpoints to help expand and deepen this concept.

When we start to examine the events happening around us, it becomes increasingly clear that we are intricately connected within an ongoing web of events. Every simple state of being has an underlying Polymaric Chain of Events (PCE) shaping it—a sequence of interlinked occurrences that influence our actions, decisions, and circumstances.

One day, I found myself at a train station, waiting for my train to college. As I had a few minutes to spare, I began contemplating my surroundings. A seemingly trivial question crossed my mind: why had I chosen to sit on this particular bench, and why by the side armrest instead of the middle? What chain of events had brought me to this exact spot, at this exact moment, and not somewhere else?

This moment of curiosity sparked the idea for the PCE theory. As I retraced my steps, I realized that my choice was influenced by multiple factors. I chose this bench because it offered shade and was slightly removed from the crowd, which itself was sparse due to the absence of nearby food stalls. Those food stalls were closed in the morning, as they only open in the evening, catering to a different crowd. The absence of morning food sales is likely due to customer demand, which reflects broader patterns of daily human activity.

Can you see how seemingly irrelevant actions and circumstances are interconnected in a web that influences my choice of seating? If the shopkeepers had been selling breakfast items, they might have kept their stalls open in the morning, attracting more people to the area. This could have made that spot busier, likely influencing me to choose a different bench altogether.

In essence, every decision and action we take is shaped by a multitude of factors and events—both significant and minor—that ripple through our lives. Recognizing this intricate network of interlinked events offers us a new way of understanding the forces that shape our daily experiences. We can see that our lives are not a collection of isolated incidents, but rather a continuous chain of interconnected moments influenced by countless variables, some of which we may never even notice.

Now, let's define some key terms needed to analyze events through the lens of the Polymaric Chain of Events (PCE) Theory.

- Chain Length

Chain length refers to the specific portion of an event's timeline under observation. While theoretically, a chain of events can extend infinitely, it is often unnecessary to trace every event back to its distant origins. Instead, we focus on a relevant slice of time, space, and subject(s) involved in the scenario.

For example, in the previous scenario where I sat on a bench at the station, we could narrow our observation to the time between when I reached the station and when I chose the bench. This defines a specific chain length for that event.

The chain length is not a simple measure of time. It consists of three dimensions:

1. **Time duration:** The period from the initial state of the first event to the final state of the last event in the

chain. It represents the span of time we're observing within the chain. In the bench example, the time might start when I arrive at the station and end when I sit down. The unit for this dimension is in seconds (SI unit: second).

2. **Place/Volume:** The physical space where the events occur. If we expand the observation area, we might include more environmental factors (like nearby shops) that contribute to the event. For example, if we analyze a few square meters of space around the bench, it would include the food stalls. If we only considered a few centimeters, we might miss these external influences. The unit for this dimension is volume (SI unit: cubic meters, m^3).

3. **Subject:** The person or object being considered in the chain of events. It could be a single individual (like me) or a group of people, animals, or even inanimate objects. The subject count is dimensionless (i.e., it has no physical unit), and is simply a numerical value representing the number of subjects involved.

The formula for chain length takes into account all three factors: time, volume, and subject count. Mathematically, it can be expressed as:

$$\text{Chain Length} = \frac{\text{Time Duration} \times \text{Volume}}{\text{Subject Count}}$$

The chain length equation

The unit for chain length, based on this formula, is seconds per cubic meter (second/m^3).

If we increase the time duration in our analysis, we capture a broader history of the event chain. For instance, if we considered the entire day leading up to my arrival at the station we would observe more factors that influenced my final decision to sit on the bench.

Increasing the spatial area allows us to include additional environmental influences. In the bench example, considering a larger volume might include other people, weather conditions, or objects that indirectly affected my choice of seating.

Increasing the number of subjects introduces more participants or objects into the event chain. For example, if we added the actions of other people sitting nearby, or even the presence of a bird on the bench, the chain becomes more complex.

Remember, chain length is a scalar unit, not a vector. Vectors have both magnitude and direction. In physics, a vector's direction is essential in describing how quantities like force, velocity, or acceleration act in space.

Chain length, as defined here, consists of a duration (time), volume (space), and subject count, but it doesn't inherently involve a specific direction in space. The concept focuses on the extent of the event chain rather than the direction in which the events unfold. Chain length measures the scale or extent of events based on time, volume, and subject, which only defines a magnitude. It quantifies how far-reaching or interconnected the events are without any directional component. Even though chain length incorporates spatial volume, it does not specify an orientation or direction within that space. Spatial extent (volume) is a scalar measure because it is simply the amount of three-dimensional space occupied, without pointing to any particular direction within that space.

Similarly, time duration and subject count are also scalar values, as they indicate quantity but do not have directional attributes. The final units of chain length, seconds per cubic meter (second/m³), reflect that the measurement is purely based on magnitudes of time, space, and count. These units don't inherently convey any directional information, supporting the interpretation of chain length as a scalar quantity.

The concept of chain length helps us frame events within specific limits that are manageable for analysis. By defining clear boundaries of time, space, and subject, we can better understand the influences that lead to any given outcome. It allows us to analyze events without getting overwhelmed by irrelevant or distant factors, offering a structured approach to tracing the cause and effect within a particular scenario.

- Event/Monomer Length:

Event or monomer length refers to the smallest measurable unit within a Polymaric Chain of Events (PCE), essentially the building block of a larger event chain. Like chain length, it is expressed using the same unit, combining time duration, spatial volume, and subject. In this context, an event is the smallest change or action that contributes to the overall sequence of events in the chain.

The concept of event chains, as described by PCE theory, spans across four dimensions: three spatial dimensions and one time dimension. This makes the event or monomer length an expression of spacetime, emphasizing that each event exists not only in a physical location but also at a specific moment in time. Therefore, it is inherently a 4D concept.

Why the PCE Theory is Bound to Four Dimensions:

1. **Space (3D):** Events occur within a volumetric space. This could be a specific point or region in the physical world (length, width, height), allowing you to understand the event's location in three-dimensional space.

2. **Time (1D):** Events are spread across a time duration, making time the fourth dimension. Each event has a start and end point, giving it a temporal aspect that is critical for understanding the progression of the chain.

3. **Bound to Spacetime:** The theory is firmly based on spacetime, meaning that all events are bound by where and when they occur. The combination of space and time in the theory makes it adaptable to most observable phenomena within our universe.

4. **Inapplicability to Higher Dimensions:** PCE theory assumes our universe exists in four dimensions, as we experience space and time. In higher-dimensional spaces (which are hypothetical or not directly observable in everyday experience), the theory may not apply because it is specifically designed to explain events within the known 4D universe.

Since event/monomer length is derived within the four-dimensional framework of spacetime, PCE theory operates within this 4D structure. It can explain most events in our observable universe but may not extend to higher-dimensional theoretical models like singularity. Thus, the theory is a comprehensive tool for analyzing events within the known four dimensions but is not equipped to handle hypothetical scenarios beyond that framework.

CHAPTER XV

Types of Event Chains

Event chains in the universe, as described by the Polymaric Chain of Events (PCE) theory, can behave in a variety of ways based on the nature of the events involved, external influences, and how they propagate through time and space. Below are some possibilities for how these chains may behave:

1. **Linear Chains:** In the simplest case, event chains can behave in a linear manner, where each event directly causes the next event in a predictable sequence. This type of event chain is often seen in deterministic processes where the outcome is almost certain based on initial conditions. A row of dominoes falling one after another in sequence, where each domino's fall directly causes the next to fall.

2. **Branching Chains:** Event chains can also branch out, meaning that one event can lead to multiple subsequent events, each following its own path. This branching could result in several chains of events happening in parallel. A person's decision to move to a new city can lead to multiple changes in their life — new friendships, job opportunities, experiences — all happening simultaneously and influencing further events in their life.

3. **Converging Chains:** In contrast to branching chains, multiple independent event chains can converge into a single event. In this case, different unrelated events from various sources all contribute to one central

outcome. A major discovery in science (e.g., the discovery of DNA) may be the result of many scientists working independently on different aspects of biology, chemistry, and physics, all of which eventually lead to the same breakthrough.

4. **Cyclic Chains:** Some event chains can form cycles, where the outcome of an event influences or triggers the starting condition of another event, creating a feedback loop. These cycles can either be positive (reinforcing the chain) or negative (damping it). Economic cycles often involve a feedback loop of events such as market crashes, recovery phases, and booms. The outcome of one economic phase triggers the next in a repeating cycle.

5. **Chaotic or Nonlinear Chains:** In certain situations, event chains can behave non-linearly, meaning small changes in one event can lead to disproportionately large or unexpected outcomes. This is similar to the concept of the "butterfly effect" in chaos theory. A small miscommunication between two people could escalate into a large argument or a breakdown of a relationship, far beyond what the initial trigger would suggest.

6. **Interconnected Webs:** Many event chains do not exist in isolation but are part of a complex web of interconnected chains. Each event can influence multiple other events, and those events, in turn, can influence others, creating a dynamic, interrelated system where everything is connected. Ecosystems operate as interconnected webs of event chains. The extinction of a species (due to hunting or habitat loss) can trigger a cascade of changes affecting the entire food chain, ecosystem balance, and even the climate.

7. **Self-Organizing Chains:** In some cases, event chains can exhibit self-organizing behavior, where a seemingly chaotic system of events organizes itself into a stable or semi-stable pattern over time, without external intervention. This behavior is often seen in systems that reach equilibrium or create emergent patterns. The formation of galaxies or planetary systems is a self-organizing chain of events, where gravity pulls matter together over time, leading to the formation of stable structures out of what was once a chaotic field of particles.

8. **Diverging and Converging Loops:** A chain can exhibit both divergence and convergence at different stages. Events may initially branch out into multiple possible outcomes, but as time progresses, they might reconverge into a single outcome due to overriding external forces or constraints. Political revolutions can start with diverse causes (economic, social, political grievances), but they might reconverge into a single significant event like the fall of a regime or establishment of a new government.

9. **Delayed Chains:** Some event chains exhibit a delayed cause-effect relationship, where the consequences of an event take time to manifest. The event may happen in the present, but the chain may only become noticeable after a significant time gap. Environmental pollution often shows delayed chains of events. Industrial pollution today might not show effects on human health or ecosystems for decades, but eventually, those effects become severe.

10. **Quantum and Probabilistic Chains:** At the quantum level, event chains may behave probabilistically, rather than deterministically. Events are not guaranteed but

are instead defined by probabilities, with multiple potential outcomes for each event. In quantum mechanics, the collapse of a quantum state into a particular observable outcome (e.g., the position of an electron) is probabilistic, and the chain of events following this collapse can take multiple potential pathways.

11. **Fractal Chains:** Some event chains could follow fractal-like patterns, where a similar type of event structure repeats on different scales. In such chains, the same event processes happen at both micro and macro levels, creating a recursive pattern. The stock market may exhibit fractal-like behavior where short-term fluctuations resemble long-term market trends, and these fluctuations can influence investor decisions at both short and long time scales.

12. **Resonant or Amplified Chains:** Certain event chains may lead to resonance where repeated similar events or influences amplify the outcome. In this case, the chain builds up energy or momentum, leading to a significant impact. Social movements often grow through resonance, where repeated acts of protest amplify public awareness and political pressure, eventually leading to large-scale changes.

13. **Parallel Chains:** Event chains can run parallel to each other without directly influencing each other. These chains develop independently, but they still exist within the same space and time. While they may not interact, their outcomes can still be part of a broader system. Two businesses in the same industry may operate independently, each following its own sequence of events, but they both contribute to the overall economy and market trends. They exist in parallel without direct

interaction.

14. **Interfering Chains:** Chains can interfere with each other, either reinforcing or disrupting the flow of events. This interaction can modify the course of each chain, leading to outcomes that neither chain would have reached independently. Two competing companies launch products at the same time. Their marketing efforts and consumer reactions will interfere, changing the success or failure of each company's product. The interaction between these chains alters the outcome for both.

15. **Cancelling Chains:** Chains can also cancel each other out, where the influence of one chain negates the effect of another. This can lead to the neutralization of outcomes that would have otherwise occurred if the chains had acted independently. In financial markets, two opposite investment strategies might cancel each other out. For instance, one group sells off a stock while another buys it in large quantities, stabilizing the price instead of allowing it to rise or fall sharply.

16. **Feedback Loops:** Chains can interact to create feedback loops, where the output of one chain feeds back into another, perpetuating the cycle. This interaction can lead to a self-reinforcing or self-correcting system. In environmental systems, increased CO_2 emissions lead to global warming, which melts polar ice caps, reducing the planet's ability to reflect sunlight and leading to further warming. This creates a reinforcing feedback loop of events.

17. **Cascading Chains:** One event chain can trigger a cascade of other chains, causing a ripple effect. A single chain can set off multiple new chains, each leading to its own outcomes, which in turn trigger more chains

in a self-expanding process. In power grids, a failure at one power plant can trigger a cascade of outages across the grid, causing other plants to shut down, resulting in a widespread blackout. The initial event chain spreads, affecting numerous systems.

18. **Dependent Chains:** Some event chains are dependent on other chains for initiation or continuation. One chain may not start or progress unless another chain has already unfolded, making them sequentially linked. Technological advancements often depend on prior discoveries. The development of modern smartphones, for instance, is dependent on earlier breakthroughs in computing, wireless communication, and materials science. One chain cannot exist without the other.

19. **Transference of Influence:** One chain may not directly affect another, but it may transfer its influence through a medium or a shared connection. For example, an intermediary event or condition can link separate chains and allow one chain's effects to propagate into another. In global politics, an event like a financial crisis in one country (Chain A) might influence the policies of another country (Chain B) through international trade agreements or economic dependencies. The chains do not directly collide, but they influence each other via the shared global market.

20. **Isolated Chains:** Some event chains remain isolated, existing without any interaction with other chains. These chains develop entirely on their own, unaffected by external events or other chains, though they still contribute to the overall structure of the universe. A person living in a remote area might lead a life where their actions (and resulting event chains) are relatively isolated from global events or social trends, though they

still exist within the larger context of the universe.

The interaction between event chains can take many forms, from merging and diverging to amplifying or cancelling out. These interactions shape the complex, dynamic behavior of systems in our universe, influencing everything from individual decisions to large-scale phenomena like climate change or societal shifts. Understanding how these chains interact provides insights into both the predictability and unpredictability of events in the world around us.

CHAPTER XVI

Law of Reference in Event Chains

The Law of Reference states that an event chain may appear different depending on the reference frame from which it is observed. This means that an event chain's behavior, connections, and interactions can vary when viewed from another person's perspective, a different time, or a different spatial location. In essence, one chain can mimic or resemble another chain, or a diverging chain may seem to be converging, based on the reference frame.

A reference frame in the context of PCE theory refers to the specific vantage point or set of conditions from which an event chain is observed or analyzed. It consists of:

1. **Observer's Perspective:** The viewpoint of the person or entity analyzing the chain. Their unique experiences, background knowledge, and position in the chain's timeline influence their perception of the chain.
2. **Time of Observation:** The specific point in time when the event chain is being examined. Observing a chain at different moments can lead to varying interpretations of how events are connected.
3. **Space:** The geographic or spatial position of the observer or the event chain itself. The spatial relationship between events may appear different when viewed from different locations.
4. **Context:** The environmental, social, or situational context that surrounds the event chain. Chains within similar contexts may seem aligned, while the same chains in different contexts may appear unrelated.

An event chain that seems unique to one observer may appear very similar to another chain when seen from a different reference frame. This could be due to the observer's position within a larger system of events, making one chain appear like another when viewed from a wider perspective. A person working in two different companies might feel like their work experiences are vastly different. However, from the reference frame of an outside observer (such as a systems analyst), the event chains (company workflows) may mimic each other closely, as both companies follow similar processes or management structures.

A single event chain can diverge into multiple paths, but from a different reference frame (such as the future or a different person's viewpoint), those diverging paths may seem to converge toward a shared outcome. A student choosing different colleges may seem to follow diverging life paths based on their choice. However, viewed from a future point in time, these different paths could converge toward the same end, such as similar career outcomes or life goals, despite taking different routes.

When two individuals observe the same event chain from different reference frames, their interpretations of the outcome can differ. One person might see an event as a failure, while another person sees it as a stepping stone for future success, based on their position in time and space. Two investors might analyze the same market trend. One who sold their stocks before a crash might view the event chain as beneficial, while another who held onto their stocks might see the same chain as disastrous. The reference frame here is their position in the timeline of events.

Each observer has their own background, knowledge, and biases, which influence how they interpret the cause-and-effect relationship of events. Depending on what they prioritize (personal gains, emotions, outcomes), they will perceive the event chain differently. Two scientists observing the same experimental result may reach different conclusions based on their theoretical frameworks. Their reference frames (scientific beliefs or paradigms) will shape how they interpret the data.

If an event chain is observed at different times, it may appear as though different processes are at work. Over time, the events in a chain can become clearer or more ambiguous, depending on the timeline. A historical event like the fall of the Roman Empire can be seen as a gradual decline when viewed over centuries, but it might appear like a sudden collapse if viewed from a specific year. Time influences how the chain is perceived.

Physical location can affect how events are perceived. Two people witnessing the same event from different places may interpret the chain of events differently due to their spatial perspective. A natural disaster like a flood may seem devastating from the affected city's point of view, while to someone observing from a faraway country, it may appear as just a regional issue. The reference frame of space changes the scale and impact of the event chain.

Context shapes the perceived importance and relevance of event chains. What seems like a critical event chain in one context may seem trivial in another. The socio-political or cultural context influences how chains interact and are valued. A local political election may seem highly significant within a small community, shaping event chains related to policy and governance. However, from a global perspective, this chain might seem less relevant compared to international events happening at the same time.

The Law of Reference highlights that event chains are not static or universally perceived in the same way. They shift and change based on the observer's reference frame, which includes their perspective, the time, space, and context in which the chain is viewed. By understanding this law, we can appreciate that what seems like diverging or converging chains to one observer might be perceived differently by another, emphasizing the complex, multifaceted nature of event chains in our universe.

CHAPTER XVII

Law of Conservation of Chain

The Law of Conservation of Chain states that an event chain can never be created or destroyed, it merely transforms from one form or type to another. This principle implies that all actions and events within the universe are part of an interconnected network, constantly shifting and evolving without ever ceasing to exist. Rather than disappearing, the energy, information, or influence within a chain is redistributed or manifests differently as new event chains.

Chains are not isolated entities but part of a continuous, interconnected web of events. When a chain appears to end, its elements are redistributed into other chains, either directly or indirectly. In this way, the impact of the original chain is preserved through transformation into a new form. A person deciding to quit their job doesn't end the chain of events related to their career. Instead, their action leads to new chains—perhaps they pursue a different career, start a business, or contribute to other people's chains in different ways.

When a chain changes form, its components (time, place, subjects) are reconfigured into different configurations, maintaining the flow of cause and effect in the system. The information or influence from one chain becomes part of others. A political movement that fades in one country may inspire or merge into another movement in a different country, preserving its core elements but changing in context and form.

Every event or action in a chain carries with it a certain amount of influence or energy. While the specifics of an event chain may transform, this influence is conserved, contributing to future actions and interactions. No event or chain loses its impact—it is simply carried forward into other chains. The invention of the internet changed the chain of human communication. While the original forms of communication (letters, phone calls) may have diminished, their influence is now embedded in new forms of digital communication, preserving the chain's legacy.

Imagine a tree in a forest that dies and falls to the ground. The tree's life can be considered one chain of events. When the tree dies, that chain does not end but transforms. Its nutrients are absorbed into the soil, contributing to the growth of new plants and trees. Animals use the fallen tree as shelter, and over time it decomposes, becoming part of the ecosystem in new ways. The original chain of the tree's life has not been destroyed; it has simply evolved into other chains of growth and decay in the forest.

CHAPTER XVIII

Chain Transformations

Event chains undergo various transformations based on interactions, reference frames, and environmental factors. These transformations can be understood as changes in the chain's characteristics, such as length, direction, or form. Here are key types of transformations:

1. **Direct Transformation:** When an event chain appears to stop, it directly leads to the formation of another chain. This is a clear cause-and-effect relationship where the end of one chain is the birth of another. A person completing their education ends the chain of being a student but directly begins the chain of their professional career.

2. **Divergent Transformation:** An event chain can split into multiple new chains, distributing its influence in different directions. These new chains may evolve independently but originate from the same source. A groundbreaking scientific discovery leads to various new research fields, technological developments, and societal changes. The original discovery's chain splits into multiple directions, each influencing different areas.

3. **Convergent Transformation:** Multiple event chains can merge into one, combining their influence into a unified chain. This often happens when different forces or elements come together to create a significant event or outcome. Different technological innovations (smartphones, cloud computing, artificial intelligence)

converge to create the modern digital economy. These originally independent chains merge to shape a larger, combined chain of influence.

The Law of Conservation of Chain works closely with the Law of Reference. Depending on the reference frame from which a chain is observed, it may appear that a chain has ended, but from a broader or different reference frame, the transformation or continuation of the chain is visible. From the perspective of an employee, resigning from a job might seem like the end of their career's chain. However, from a future perspective or from an outsider's view, this could simply be the beginning of a new, transformative chain leading to a different job or career path.

The law implies that every action or event in the universe has lasting consequences. Even when events seem to fade into insignificance, their influence lingers and becomes part of new chains, preserving the continuity of cause and effect. Since chains can transform but not be destroyed, everything in the universe is interconnected. Events, people, places, and time are woven together in a seamless web of transformations, making it impossible to isolate any one event completely from the whole. While the transformation of chains follows a natural flow, the exact way in which they will change form can be unpredictable. Since chains can split, merge, or evolve in complex ways, predicting the future course of an event chain can be difficult. A small act of kindness may ripple through society, influencing people and events in ways that the original actor could never have predicted. The chain of events transforms, but its influence continues in unexpected forms.

The Law of Conservation of Chain provides a framework to understand the ongoing flow of cause and effect in the universe. It asserts that while chains of events may change form, their essence—their influence, time, space, and subjects—are never lost. By understanding that chains only transform, not disappear, we gain a deeper appreciation for the perpetual interconnectedness of all things and the ways in which even seemingly insignificant events continue to influence the world long after they appear to end.

CHAPTER XIX

Mathematical Calculations with PCE

In Polymaric Chain of Events (PCE) theory, mathematical calculations can help us analyze and quantify the dynamics of event chains, their interactions, and transformations. Here are a few examples of the possible mathematical calculations within the PCE framework:

1. Chain Length Calculation:

As discussed earlier, the chain length in PCE is defined as:

$$L = \frac{T \times V}{N}$$

T = Time duration of the chain (in seconds), V = Volume (spatial region) affected by the chain (in cubic meters, m³), N = Number of subjects (entities) involved in the chain (dimensionless)

- Example Calculation:

Imagine you're analyzing an event chain where you were seated on a train station bench for 30 minutes (1800 seconds). The spatial region affected by the chain is approximately 10 square meters (considering the bench, nearby area, and other factors like the stalls and crowd). You're the only subject in the chain. The chain length L can be calculated as:

$$L = \frac{T \times V}{N} = \frac{1800 \times 10}{1} = 18,000 \, \text{sec/m}^3$$

This gives us the "length" or magnitude of this event chain in the units of sec/m³.

2. Monomer Length Calculation:
Each event within a larger chain can be broken down into smaller "monomers" (individual events). Monomer length is simply a segment of the chain length and can be computed similarly.

- Example Calculation:

If a sub-event (e.g., moving from standing near the station entrance to the bench) took 300 seconds (5 minutes) and occupied a volume of 2 m³, and you are still the only subject, then the monomer length would be:

$$L_{\text{monomer}} = \frac{300 \times 2}{1} = 600 \, \text{sec}/\text{m}^3$$

3. Chain Overlap and Interaction:
When two or more chains interact, we can calculate their **overlap volume** and time duration to understand how intertwined they are. The **interaction index** can be computed as the percentage of overlap between the chains.

- Example Calculation:

If Chain A has a volume of 20 m³ and duration of 1,200 seconds, and Chain B has a volume of 15 m³ and duration of 1,500 seconds, the overlap between the two might occupy 5 m³ and a time overlap of 600 seconds. The interaction index I can be calculated as:

$$I = \frac{\text{Overlap Volume} \times \text{Overlap Time}}{\text{Chain A Volume} \times \text{Chain A Time}} \times 100$$

$$I = \frac{5 \times 600}{20 \times 1200} \times 100 = 12.5\%$$

This shows that 12.5% of Chain A's length overlaps with Chain B. This could be useful in analyzing how much two events or actions influenced each other.

4. Chain Convergence/Divergence Rates:

If event chains converge or diverge over time, we can calculate the **rate of convergence or divergence** to determine how fast these transformations occur.

- Example Calculation:

If two event chains (A and B) are converging, the spatial distance between them reduces over time. Suppose at time t=0, they are 100 meters apart, and at t=200 seconds, they are 40 meters apart. The rate of convergence would be:

$$R_c = \frac{\text{Initial Distance} - \text{Final Distance}}{\text{Time Interval}} = \frac{100 - 40}{200} = 0.3\,\text{m/s}$$

This means that the chains are converging at a rate of 0.3 meters per second.

5. Probability of Chain Interaction:

In some cases, it might be useful to calculate the **probability** of two chains interacting based on their spatial and temporal proximity. The interaction probability Pinteraction can be calculated as a function of overlap in time, volume, and subject involvement.

$$P_{\text{interaction}} = \frac{T_{\text{overlap}}}{T_{\text{total}}} \times \frac{V_{\text{overlap}}}{V_{\text{total}}}$$

- Example Calculation:

If two chains have a time overlap of 300 seconds and their total duration is 1000 seconds, with a volume overlap of 8 m³ out of a total volume of 20 m³, the probability of interaction is:

$$P_{\text{interaction}} = \frac{300}{1000} \times \frac{8}{20} = 0.12 = 12\%$$

This tells us that there is a 12% chance that these chains will significantly interact.

6. Chain Evolution: Growth Rate:

Chains can evolve and grow in both time and volume, particularly as events become more complex or gather more subjects. The **growth rate** of a chain can be computed by examining how the chain's length changes over time.

- Example Calculation:

If an event chain initially occupies a volume of 5 m³ and, after 100 seconds, grows to a volume of 25 m³, we can compute the growth rate as:

$$\text{Growth Rate} = \frac{V_{\text{final}} - V_{\text{initial}}}{T_{\text{final}} - T_{\text{initial}}} = \frac{25 - 5}{100 - 0} = 0.2\,\text{m}^3/\text{sec}$$

This gives us the rate at which the chain's spatial influence is expanding.

Summary of Potential Calculations in PCE:

- **Chain Length:**

$$L = \frac{T \times V}{N}$$

T = Time duration of the chain (in seconds), V = Volume (spatial region) affected by the chain (in cubic meters, m^3), N = Number of subjects (entities) involved in the chain (dimensionless)

- **Monomer Length:** Subdivision of the chain length into smaller events.
- **Interaction Index:** Measures the extent of overlap between two chains.
- **Convergence/Divergence Rate:** Quantifies how fast event chains move toward or away from each other.
- **Probability of Interaction:** Based on spatial and temporal overlap.
- **Chain Growth Rate:** Measures how quickly an event chain evolves or expands in space and time.

These calculations provide a mathematical framework to understand and quantify event chains, helping us explore the complexity of interactions, transformations, and growth of events in the universe.

Unite: The Rational Society

CHAPTER XX

The Rational Sweet Point

When we discuss rationalism, it's common to encounter the assumption—either from others or from within ourselves—that being rational often equates to being less moral. While it's true that rational thinking can sometimes lead to decisions that seem to compromise ethical considerations, this isn't always the case. Rationality and morality are not inherently opposed. In fact, upon closer examination, ethical or moral decisions often have their own form of rationality embedded within them.

For instance, consider the scenario of two nations locked in constant conflict. From a purely strategic standpoint, it might seem rational to use nuclear power to gain a decisive victory. However, when you factor in the long-term consequences—post-war recovery, human suffering, global peace, and environmental destruction—the ethical stance against nuclear war also has its own rational basis. It considers the broader picture, where the survival of humanity and future stability take precedence over short-term military gains.

Another example can be seen in everyday decision-making. Take the debate on healthcare: some might argue that from a financial perspective, limiting healthcare to those who can afford it is rational, as it conserves resources and minimizes government expenditure. But an ethical approach, which considers the well-being and dignity of all individuals, also has rational merit. A healthier population contributes to a more productive society, reducing long-term healthcare costs and social instability. Thus, morality in this case aligns with rationality when viewed through a broader lens.

A similar situation arises in environmental conservation. It might seem rational to exploit natural resources for immediate economic benefit. However, the ethical standpoint, which emphasizes the responsibility to protect the environment for future generations, is rational when we consider the long-term impacts of environmental degradation on human survival, health, and the economy.

Rationality, by definition, is the process of evaluating all possible options and selecting the most logical, practical, and effective path. If we were to plot two seemingly opposing ideologies on a two-dimensional graph—each having its own valid points, supported by logical and justifiable arguments—we would likely find that the most practical solution lies somewhere in the middle, forming a bell curve of possibilities.

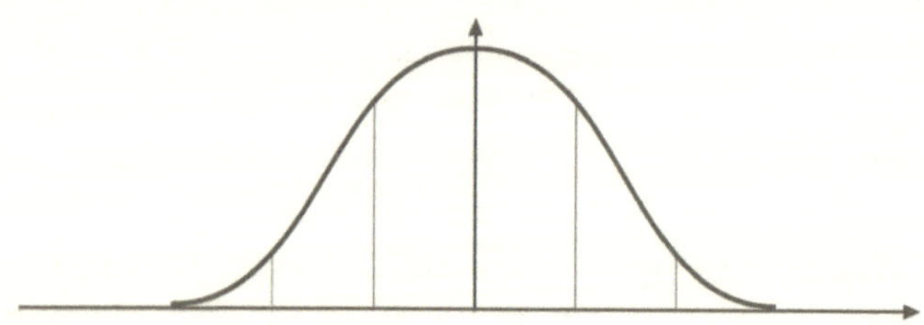

Bell curve

Consider the example of war again. On one side, hawkish proponents may argue that a preemptive strike on an adversary is the best defense. They might downplay or ignore considerations like human suffering, civilian casualties, and the economic fallout of war. On the other side, pacifists may argue that avoiding conflict at all costs is the moral high ground, emphasizing peace and diplomacy, yet failing to recognize that inaction could lead to oppression or further violence. Both positions have logical underpinnings. The optimal solution, however, is likely a balance between the two, one that incorporates both defensive actions and efforts to preserve peace. This balanced approach is both ethical and rational, as it takes into account all possible consequences, both immediate and long-term.

Another powerful example is in the realm of criminal justice. Some argue that harsh punishments for criminals are the most rational way to deter crime, focusing on the logic of strict retribution. On the other hand, others advocate for rehabilitation over punishment, emphasizing the ethical imperative to provide individuals with opportunities for redemption. The most rational approach may be a combination of both—ensuring justice is served while also offering a path for rehabilitation, reducing the likelihood of repeat offenses. This balanced solution merges ethical considerations with rational outcomes.

These examples demonstrate that rationality and morality are not necessarily at odds with one another. When all possible outcomes and consequences are properly considered, they often converge. The key lies in finding what we can call the "sweet spot" of rationality—where logical reasoning and ethical integrity align, leading to decisions that are both practical and morally sound.

In my journey through life, I have encountered many people who identify themselves as rational thinkers. However, at certain moments or in specific situations, they tend to stray from their rational mindset and embrace an irrational one. The opposite also holds true—those who generally act irrationally may, on occasion, display a surprising level of rational thought.

For example, a well-educated person with a solid understanding of the laws of physics might still reject scientific explanations when it comes to the origins of the Earth, preferring instead to embrace the belief that it was created by a divine entity. Despite possessing the knowledge to approach this topic logically, they choose to set aside their rationality and follow a path rooted in faith or tradition.

Similarly, a person who passionately advocates for the equality of all human beings might compromise that belief when faced with a situation involving a specific religion or community. They may allow isolated, negative experiences to cloud their judgment, leading them to act irrationally, treating people from that group unfairly despite their foundational belief in equality.

This is a dangerous and critical state of mind, one that we must actively identify and avoid. It represents a moment where a person is no longer driven by rational thought or ethical considerations, but by pure irrationality. In this state, logic and morality are abandoned, and ego or biases take over.

A truly rational person would adhere to what we might call the "bell curve" of balanced thinking, constantly striving to maintain equilibrium in their judgment. Such a person would not be led astray by ego, prejudice, or emotional impulses. They would not only be willing to listen to opposing viewpoints but would also actively evaluate them with an open mind. A rational thinker possesses the self-awareness to recognize when irrationality or ego begins to take hold, allowing them to recalibrate their mindset and steer themselves back toward reason.

To maintain this balance, it's crucial to remain vigilant and reflective, constantly questioning whether our decisions are being shaped by reason or whether external factors—biases, emotions, or societal pressures—are leading us astray. Rationality, at its core, requires not just the capacity to think logically, but the humility to admit when we are drifting into irrational territory.

In our previous discussions on PCE theory, we explored how our understanding of the universe is deeply rooted in space and time. When seeking the "sweet point" of rationalism, it's essential to recognize that time plays a critical role here as well. The term "bell curve" arises from the shape of the distribution when two opposing factors are plotted on a simple two-dimensional graph. However, real-life decisions are rarely confined to just two dimensions. They are, in fact, multi-dimensional, involving numerous variables beyond just a pair of competing perspectives.

Take, for example, the case of war that we previously discussed. Finding the rational sweet spot in this scenario cannot be done by merely considering two extremes—say, hawkish aggression versus pacifist restraint. Time itself becomes a critical axis to consider. Within a fixed time frame, it might appear that a nuclear strike offers the most rational solution in the immediate short term (perhaps as a deterrent or defense strategy). Yet, if we extend that timeline, we may realize that in the longer term, other solutions—such as diplomacy or economic sanctions—emerge as more rational and sustainable choices. Therefore, time profoundly influences how rationality is perceived in this multi-dimensional space.

The rationalist's goal, then, should not be to simply balance two opposing ideas but to navigate a complex, multi-dimensional space where numerous axes, such as ethics, long-term consequences, practicality, and—most importantly—time are factored into every decision. Rationality becomes more than just a trade-off between extremes; it becomes a dynamic process of weighing possibilities across these diverse axes.

Let's consider another example. Faith, while often critiqued for its adverse effects on rational thinking, cannot be abolished or discredited through immediate force or abrupt measures. If we only consider rationality in a static, short-term context, we may push too aggressively, causing social unrest or backlash. Instead, by integrating time as an essential input, we understand that the path toward a more rational society may require gradual shifts. Over time, education, discourse, and cultural evolution can guide humanity toward this rational sweet point. In this way, rationalism needs time to manifest its full effects, and forcing change without allowing time for adaptation may, in itself, be irrational.

Ultimately, rationality is not a static point to be found in a two-dimensional plane but a constantly evolving sweet spot that needs to be approached slowly, taking into account all relevant dimensions—including time. This nuanced understanding prevents irrational extremes and allows rationality to align with ethicality, practicality, and the realities of human society.

CHAPTER XXI

Pillars of a Rational Society

Now that we have identified our adversary—faith—and understood the psychological effects that reinforce faith-based and other irrational beliefs, we can also recognize the manipulation techniques used to maintain these mindsets. We've explored the fabric of the universe through PCE theory and learned how to maintain a balanced, unbiased, and rational perspective in decision-making. With these tools in hand, we are now ready to discuss how to build a truly rational society.

While the advancement of technology and science has indeed spread rational thought more widely than ever before, faith-based distractions—such as religion, superstition, and inequality—have also evolved to adapt to modern times. Religious conservatism, for instance, now uses social media to spread inequality and discrimination, while astrology apps and businesses promoting pseudoscience are thriving in today's market.

In order to form a truly rational society, there are two essential principles we need to understand:

- **Irrationality must be tackled from its root:** True rationality must be cultivated within people. It must come from their own understanding and critical thinking, not imposed externally.
- **Existing societies cannot be fundamentally changed:** Instead of trying to overhaul the current societal structure, the focus should be on forming new societies with like-minded individuals, where rational thinking is

the foundation.

Society is like the ocean. As an individual, you cannot create massive waves by merely jumping into it. Instead, you can create your own smaller body of water, governed by your rational principles. If your rational society prospers, others will be drawn to it organically. Over time, as more people question the validity of their faith-based ideologies, they may join you. If successful, your rational society can grow and even overlap with the old, irrational society.

This is how religion historically gained dominance: it started with small, like-minded communities and expanded over centuries by refining its process. Rationalism has never had a clearly defined path to follow. Scientific discoveries, while revolutionary, have been isolated efforts, yet they have changed the world significantly. If we establish a well-defined, organized rational society, it can bring about an unprecedented level of advancement.

After much reflection, I have identified nine key pillars essential for creating a rational society. These pillars represent core areas where we need to focus in order to cultivate a community in which faith-based ideologies become obsolete, people are equipped to identify psychological manipulations, and they can guard themselves against irrational thinking. In the current context of India, here are the pillars:

1. **Education Over Literacy:** True education is about critical thinking, not just the ability to read and write. Rationality stems from a deep understanding of knowledge, not rote learning.

2. **Empower Women in Rationalism:** Women's empowerment is critical to creating a rational society. A society that empowers women to think critically will elevate rational thought for all.

3. Strong Environmental Awareness: Rationality includes understanding the impact of human actions on the environment. People must be aware of how to make sustainable decisions for the future of our planet.

4. **Develop Positive Human Ethics:** Ethics grounded in rationality lead to fairness, justice, and equality. Rationality should encourage people to prioritize human welfare over superstition and discrimination.

5. **Support and Motivate Creativity:** Creativity is the key to innovation and progress. A rational society should nurture and encourage the creative potential of its members to solve problems and advance knowledge.

6. **Preserve Diverse Cultural Heritage:** Rationalism does not mean abandoning culture. Instead, it's about appreciating diverse cultural heritages in a way that celebrates human creativity and history, without falling into the traps of irrational dogma.

7. **Mental and Physical Health Awareness:** A rational society must prioritize both mental and physical health. Awareness in these areas helps individuals make informed choices for their well-being and fosters a healthier community overall.

8. **Time and Money Management Skill Development:** Rational decision-making extends to practical aspects of life such as managing time and money effectively. These skills are crucial for personal success and the advancement of society as a whole.

9. **Normalize Educational Qualification in Politics:** Political leaders should have a solid educational

foundation, as their decisions shape society. This pillar emphasizes the importance of rational thinking in governance.

These nine pillars form the foundation of a rational society. By focusing on these areas, we can create a community where faith-based beliefs naturally lose their appeal, and individuals are empowered to think critically, act ethically, and thrive in a world guided by reason.

- Education Over Literacy

The divide between literacy and education is one of the most critical issues we face when working towards a rational society. While technological advancements and improved infrastructure have made literacy more accessible, the essence of true education—critical thinking and rational decision-making—is not always instilled in individuals. This gap is particularly evident in societies that, despite their literacy rates, are still dominated by irrational beliefs, superstitions, and faith-based ideologies.

From the research I've conducted, it is clear that individuals who struggle to think rationally often lack a strong rational foundation in their early upbringing. The problem usually stems from two key areas:

1. **Family Environment:** MostIndian households tend to be religious and faith-based by default. Children are often exposed to rituals, superstitions, and religious doctrines from a very young age. This constant exposure creates a cognitive framework where faith-based reasoning becomes second nature, making it difficult for rational thought to take root.

2. **Educational Institutions:** Schools and educational systems, which should ideally counterbalance this faith-based upbringing, often fail to do so. Instead of promoting critical thinking and rationality, schools focus on subjects as tools for competition—encouraging rote memorization and exam-based learning, rather than nurturing independent thought and inquiry. This leaves students vulnerable to irrational beliefs, as they are not equipped with the mental tools to question or defend against faith-based influences.

A small fraction of individuals who consistently make rational decisions often come from environments where rational thinking was encouraged during their formative years. Whether through exceptional schools, rational parents, or external influences, these individuals developed strong mental frameworks that protected them from faith-based thinking. This early influence is crucial, as the mind is most malleable in childhood, and any exposure to irrational ideas can lead to lifelong habits of faith-based reasoning.

The solution, therefore, lies in changing the educational system to focus on overall human development rather than simply teaching subjects. Schools should not only teach mathematics, physics, or languages but also introduce students to concepts like how misinformation spreads and recognizing manipulation in everyday life and the cognitive biases, mental fallacies, and how human emotions can distort logical thinking. They should encourage children to approach problems with a scientific mindset and focus on evidence-based conclusions.

To bridge the gap between literacy and true education, we need to shift our educational focus towards practical learning and rational decision-making. Instead of solely relying on theoretical knowledge, students should be exposed to real-world scenarios where they can apply what they've learned and are challenged to think critically.

One potential solution is to introduce a **Student Rationality Index**—a metric designed to measure how well students can apply rational thinking in real-life situations. This index would be assessed through scenario-based tests that measure how a student responds to challenges that may conflict with cultural or religious beliefs.

For example, imagine a scenario in which a student is confronted with a common superstition: a black cat is injured on the side of the road, and the student is aware of the cultural belief that black cats bring bad luck. In this test, the student's response would be evaluated to determine whether they choose to help the injured animal or whether they are influenced by superstition. The student's Rationality Index score would reflect how well they can navigate such situations, using logic and compassion rather than falling back on irrational beliefs.

This index could be applied throughout a student's educational journey, from school to college, and even into their working environment. It would provide a continuous measure of their ability to think rationally and make evidence-based decisions in everyday life.

The only way to truly close the gap between literacy and education is to embed rational thinking into the core of the curriculum, starting from early childhood. Students must be taught about cognitive biases and how external influences shape our thoughts. The curiosity, skepticism, and the importance of asking "why" before accepting beliefs should be encouraged and shift the focus on compassion, fairness, and equity in a rational, evidence-based framework.

Schools should regularly test and observe how well students apply these teachings in practical scenarios. This would create a generation of individuals capable of evaluating their own thoughts, questioning societal norms, and embracing rationality at every turn.

Without embedding rational thought into our education system, we risk producing generations of literate people who can recite facts but cannot challenge the superstitions or manipulations that plague society. The education system must shift from teaching subjects for competition's sake to teaching students how to live as rational, critical-thinking beings.

This is why the pillar of **Education Over Literacy** is the foundation for a rational society. It equips individuals with the tools they need to guard against irrationality and faith-based thinking, promoting a society that can think for itself, free from the constraints of superstition, manipulation, and dogma.

- Empower Women in Rationalism

Women in India have long been subjected to patriarchal and faith-based systems, which have limited their intellectual and personal growth. From birth, women in many Indian households are exposed to gendered teachings deeply rooted in religious dogma and cultural traditions. These teachings often reinforce the idea that women should conform to subservient roles, uphold irrational beliefs, and avoid questioning the status quo. This conditioning creates a barrier to rational thought, making women more susceptible to manipulation and control through faith-based ideologies.

Although there has been progress in women's education in recent decades, the quality of education—particularly its capacity to encourage critical thinking and rationalism—remains limited. Educational efforts are often undermined by the pervasive influence of patriarchal cultural norms, religious dogma, and societal expectations, which hinder the development of an independent and rational mindset among women.

Given this context, empowering women in rationalism is not just about providing education in the conventional sense; it involves dismantling the deep-rooted faith-based and patriarchal structures that restrict women's intellectual freedom. Below are some strategies and examples of how we can empower women in rationalism and help them break free from these constraints.

The most direct way to empower women in rationalism is through education reform. However, merely increasing literacy or formal education is not enough. There needs to be a shift in the quality of education offered to girls and women—one that promotes critical thinking, scientific reasoning, and independence of thought.

Schools and educational institutions should integrate rational thinking and critical analysis as core components of the curriculum, especially in girls' schools. Subjects like philosophy, ethics, and logic should be introduced early, with a focus on questioning dogma and understanding the world through evidence-based reasoning. In Kerala, the "Student Police Cadet" program encourages girls to take part in community policing and problem-solving activities. These activities develop critical thinking, leadership skills, and a sense of responsibility, encouraging girls to question existing norms and practices. Teachers, especially female teachers, should be trained to encourage independent thinking among students. They should help girls challenge patriarchal or religious assumptions in the curriculum and their lives.

Women in India often lack safe spaces where they can express their thoughts freely, question societal norms, or challenge faith-based dogma without fear of retribution. Establishing such spaces, both physical and digital, can provide women with opportunities to develop their rational thinking. Creating small, community-based women's study circles can provide platforms for women to come together and discuss issues like rationalism, gender equality, and science. These circles should emphasize critical thinking and provide resources on philosophical and scientific topics that challenge faith-based dogma. Digital platforms can be an excellent way to empower women in rationalism. Online forums, discussion groups, and social media communities can be designed specifically for women to discuss rational ideas, challenge superstitions, and support one another in developing critical thinking skills. This is particularly valuable for women in conservative families who may not have access to such discussions offline.

Representation matters, especially when it comes to fostering rationalism in women. Women need to see examples of female leaders in science, philosophy, and rational thought to inspire them to question the world around them and challenge irrational beliefs. Showcasing Female Rationalist Leaders: Schools, media, and public institutions should highlight the contributions of women in rational thought, science, and innovation. This could be done through documentaries, seminars, or campaigns that showcase women like Savitribai Phule, India's first female teacher and social reformer, or modern women scientists like Dr. Tessy Thomas, the 'Missile Woman of India.'

Economic independence and political participation are key factors in developing a rational mindset. Women who are economically independent are less likely to rely on traditional or religious structures that promote subservience, and they are more empowered to think critically and make independent decisions. Similarly, political participation allows women to engage in public discourse and policy-making that challenge irrational societal norms. Providing women with skills and education that lead to financial independence is crucial. This independence allows women to break free from faith-based dependency structures often controlled by patriarchal systems. Training programs that focus on modern technology, entrepreneurship, and leadership should be made accessible to women across socio-economic backgrounds. SEWA (Self-Employed Women's Association) in Gujarat provides training to rural women in various skills, helping them gain economic independence. Many of these women go on to question traditional practices that kept them in poverty, thus fostering a sense of rational autonomy.

Women's involvement in politics can help bring rational policies to the forefront of public discourse, particularly on issues such as education reform, healthcare, and gender equality. Female political leaders who advocate for rationalism can inspire societal change on a larger scale.

Media plays an enormous role in shaping societal norms and ideas. Unfortunately, many mainstream media outlets in India perpetuate religious and patriarchal narratives that reinforce women's subordination. Media reform is essential for empowering women in rationalism.

Television shows, films, and web series should depict women as independent thinkers and challenge the gender roles traditionally imposed by faith-based systems. This content can be entertaining yet informative, helping to shift public opinion gradually. The web series "Satyamev Jayate" took on topics like superstition, dowry, and domestic violence, using real-life stories to question faith-based practices. It sparked national debates and encouraged viewers to think critically about irrational customs, particularly those affecting women.

Women should be encouraged to consume media that promotes critical thinking and rationality. Educational campaigns can raise awareness about the manipulative nature of faith-based and patriarchal narratives in popular media.

Empowering women in rationalism is not just about education but about transforming societal structures that perpetuate irrational beliefs. It requires reforming education, creating safe spaces for discussion, promoting female role models in rationalism, encouraging economic and political independence, and using media as a tool for change. Only by empowering women in these areas can we break the cycle of faith-based patriarchy and create a society where women are free to think, question, and contribute to the advancement of rational thought.

• Strong Environmental Awareness

A rational society must recognize the importance of environmental sustainability. Rationality isn't just about logic in human interactions but also in how we interact with the planet. A society that understands the science of climate change, deforestation, and biodiversity loss will make more informed decisions about resource consumption and conservation. Environmental awareness is essential for long-term survival and prosperity. By fostering a rational understanding of our ecosystems, people will adopt more sustainable lifestyles, such as reducing waste, conserving energy, and supporting renewable resources. Rational environmental decisions also involve weighing short-term gains against long-term consequences, ensuring the well-being of future generations.

One of the most effective strategies for fostering environmental awareness is through education and community outreach. Schools and universities can integrate environmental science, climate change, and sustainability into their curriculums from an early age. For example, schools in Finland teach students about recycling, conservation, and the importance of reducing carbon footprints as part of their environmental education. Community-driven programs can also be implemented to educate adults and children on sustainable living practices, such as water conservation, tree planting, and reducing plastic usage. The "Eco-Schools" initiative, which operates in many countries worldwide, is an excellent example of how education can lead to improved environmental awareness among young people.

Governments play a critical role in enforcing environmental sustainability through policies and regulations that limit harmful activities and incentivize sustainable practices. For example, Costa Rica has been hailed as a global leader in environmental policy. Over 98% of its energy comes from renewable sources, and it has implemented national programs to reforest degraded areas, which has led to a dramatic increase in forest cover. Another example is the European Union's "Green Deal," which aims to make Europe the first climate-neutral continent by 2050. The policy includes regulations for reducing carbon emissions, improving energy efficiency, and promoting circular economies.

Many businesses are increasingly integrating sustainability into their corporate strategy, contributing to environmental awareness. Companies like Patagonia and IKEA have been at the forefront of promoting sustainable practices in their industries. Patagonia donates 1% of its sales to environmental causes and encourages consumers to repair and recycle their products instead of buying new ones. IKEA is investing heavily in renewable energy and aims to become climate positive by 2030. These corporate strategies not only contribute to environmental sustainability but also raise awareness among consumers and other businesses.

Urban planning can have a major impact on environmental sustainability. The development of eco-friendly cities, where green energy, waste reduction, and sustainable transportation options are prioritized, can significantly raise environmental awareness. For instance, the city of Copenhagen in Denmark has committed to becoming carbon-neutral by 2025. It has invested in extensive cycling infrastructure, renewable energy, and public transport systems that reduce the city's carbon footprint. These urban design strategies not only create sustainable living environments but also educate the public about the practical benefits of environmental stewardship.

Grassroots movements driven by citizens can be powerful agents for raising environmental awareness and driving change. Greta Thunberg's "Fridays for Future" movement, which began as a lone protest against climate inaction, quickly grew into a global movement involving millions of young people across the world. This grassroots initiative has significantly raised awareness about the urgency of addressing climate change and has pressured governments to take action. Another example is India's "Chipko Movement" from the 1970s, where rural villagers, mostly women, protested deforestation by hugging trees to prevent them from being cut down. This movement helped raise awareness about forest conservation in India and contributed to the implementation of stricter forest protection laws.

Encouraging sustainable agricultural practices is another vital strategy. Organic farming, permaculture, and agroforestry are examples of farming techniques that promote soil health, reduce water consumption, and minimize the use of harmful pesticides. The "Zero Budget Natural Farming" (ZBNF) initiative in India, championed by Subhash Palekar, is an example of a sustainable farming practice that has gained traction. It emphasizes using natural resources to maintain crop yields without relying on expensive chemicals. ZBNF has helped many farmers reduce their input costs and produce food more sustainably, raising awareness of environmentally conscious agricultural practices.

Governments and businesses can provide incentives for the use of renewable energy sources, such as solar, wind, and hydropower, to reduce reliance on fossil fuels. The German "Energiewende" policy is a real-world example of how a country can promote renewable energy on a large scale. Germany has introduced subsidies and incentives for solar and wind energy, which have made it a leader in the renewable energy transition. As of 2020, more than 40% of Germany's electricity was generated from renewable sources, significantly raising public awareness of the environmental benefits of clean energy.

Partnerships between governments, NGOs, and private corporations can create impactful environmental awareness campaigns. For instance, "The Ocean Cleanup" project, a non-profit supported by various organizations, aims to remove plastic waste from oceans using advanced technologies. The initiative has raised global awareness about the plastic pollution crisis, while also providing tangible solutions. Similarly, the WWF's "Earth Hour" campaign, where millions of people worldwide turn off their lights for one hour to raise awareness about energy conservation, is an excellent example of how public and private partnerships can bring environmental issues to the forefront.

Rwanda's government implemented one of the most successful plastic bag bans in the world. In 2008, Rwanda completely banned the use of plastic bags, which has significantly improved the country's environmental health. The ban is strictly enforced, and violators face heavy fines or even jail time. As a result, Rwanda's streets and landscapes are notably cleaner, and the government has raised environmental awareness about the dangers of plastic pollution. This bold move has inspired other nations in Africa and around the world to take similar measures.

- Develop Positive Human Ethics

Ethics grounded in rationality focus on promoting fairness, justice, and equality in society. Rational thinking leads to ethical decisions that benefit humanity as a whole, rather than being influenced by superstition, biases, or historical inequalities. For instance, rational ethics reject discrimination based on race, gender, or religion, and instead advocate for equal opportunities for all individuals.

Rationality also encourages an evidence-based approach to solving social issues, from healthcare to poverty alleviation. By building a society where human welfare is prioritized over harmful traditions or superstitions, rational ethics can help create a more just and compassionate world. Teaching children not only the principles of right and wrong but also the reasoning behind those principles will help them make informed, compassionate decisions as they grow. For instance, Finland's education system includes subjects like social and emotional learning, which help students understand empathy, collaboration, and fairness. Schools can integrate lessons on rational decision-making, anti-discrimination practices, and the importance of equality, laying the foundation for ethical thinking.

Another strategy to achieve this is through experiential learning activities, such as community service projects, where individuals engage directly with diverse social groups. This experience can help people break free from stereotypes and develop a deeper understanding of others' struggles. For example, in Denmark, social integration programs bring together students from different socio-economic backgrounds, fostering empathy and cooperation. Encouraging debate and open discussion in schools and workplaces on ethical dilemmas can also help individuals think critically and adopt ethical principles based on reason rather than dogma or tradition.

Governments, institutions, and civil society must work together to raise awareness about human rights and their importance in maintaining fairness and justice. Campaigns led by organizations like Amnesty International and the United Nations Human Rights Council play a vital role in promoting global human rights and holding individuals and governments accountable. By educating the public on these rights, societies can shift towards ethical standards that prioritize equality, dignity, and mutual respect.

Many unethical practices are rooted in long-standing cultural and religious biases. A rational approach to ethics involves actively dismantling these biases and replacing them with values that promote inclusion and equality. Governments can introduce policies that enforce anti-discrimination laws in schools, workplaces, and public spaces. For example, South Africa's post-apartheid constitution emphasizes equality and protection from discrimination based on race, gender, or religion. Implementing strong legal frameworks and awareness campaigns can help break down the cultural barriers that perpetuate inequality and injustice.

Leaders—whether in government, business, or community organizations—should be held to ethical standards that prioritize the well-being of people and the planet. Transparency and accountability are key strategies to ensure ethical leadership. Initiatives like the "Global Compact" by the United Nations encourage businesses to adopt sustainable and ethical practices, while many countries have established anti-corruption watchdogs to ensure public officials are held accountable for their actions. By encouraging ethical leadership, society can promote fairness and justice at all levels.

Ethical journalism and media literacy programs can help people discern factual, balanced reporting from manipulative or biased content. For instance, the Ethical Journalism Network promotes standards for news organizations to follow, ensuring that journalism is based on truth, fairness, and integrity. Media literacy initiatives, like those seen in Finland and Canada, educate people about identifying misinformation and bias in news and social media. These programs empower individuals to make rational ethical judgments based on accurate information.

One notable example of fostering positive human ethics is South Africa's Truth and Reconciliation Commission (TRC) after the end of apartheid. This commission aimed to bring justice, healing, and accountability by exposing the atrocities committed during apartheid and offering a platform for both victims and perpetrators to be heard. The TRC was based on principles of restorative justice, where reconciliation and truth were prioritized over revenge or punishment. This approach, grounded in empathy, accountability, and fairness, helped South Africa transition toward a more ethical and equitable society, setting a precedent for post-conflict reconciliation worldwide.

- Support and Motivate Creativity

Creativity is the lifeblood of innovation and progress. A rational society should not only embrace but also actively encourage creativity in all its forms—whether in art, science, or technology. Rational thinking supports creative problem-solving by providing a structured way to think outside the box and explore new possibilities. For example, fostering creativity in education by encouraging inquiry and experimentation rather than rote learning allows students to think critically and innovate. Rational creativity helps push boundaries, finding new solutions to existing problems while enriching culture and knowledge.

By integrating creative arts, critical thinking exercises, and problem-solving activities into the curriculum, schools can provide students with the tools they need to think outside the box. For instance, project-based learning allows students to collaborate on real-world issues, encouraging them to apply their knowledge creatively. In countries like Finland, where education emphasizes creativity, students are encouraged to explore their interests and passions, leading to higher engagement and innovative thinking. This approach contrasts with rote memorization and standardized testing, which often stifle creativity.

To foster creativity, it's essential to create collaborative environments where individuals can share ideas and learn from one another. Co-working spaces, innovation hubs, and makerspaces provide platforms for collaboration, experimentation, and interdisciplinary projects. The Co-creation Hub in Nigeria is a community-driven innovation center that brings together entrepreneurs, artists, and tech enthusiasts to collaborate on projects that address local challenges. These spaces not only inspire creativity but also facilitate networking and the exchange of diverse perspectives.

Providing funding, grants, and resources for artists, writers, filmmakers, and musicians can help nurture creative talent and foster innovation. UK's Creative Industries Council works to promote the creative sector by advocating for policies that support artists and creative businesses, recognizing their economic and cultural impact. By investing in creative industries, societies can harness the power of creativity to drive economic development and social change.

Organizations should encourage employees to explore new ideas and approaches, even if they lead to failure. Google's "20% Time" policy, which allows employees to spend 20% of their work hours on passion projects, has led to innovations like Gmail and Google News. Similarly, companies like IDEO and Pixar foster a culture of creativity by encouraging brainstorming sessions and collaborative workshops where all ideas are valued. By promoting a safe environment for experimentation, organizations can unlock the creative potential of their workforce.

When individuals from various backgrounds and experiences come together, they bring unique perspectives that can inspire innovative ideas. Organizations should prioritize diversity in hiring practices and create inclusive spaces where everyone feels valued and heard. Initiatives like the Diversity in Tech movement aim to increase representation of underrepresented groups in the tech industry, recognizing that diverse teams lead to more creative solutions. Celebrating diversity in all its forms helps cultivate a rich creative landscape.

Tools like design software, online collaboration platforms, and social media can help individuals and teams brainstorm, prototype, and share their ideas more effectively. Platforms like Behance and Dribbble allow artists and designers to showcase their work and connect with potential collaborators. Additionally, artificial intelligence (AI) tools, such as DALL-E and ChatGPT, can aid in generating ideas and exploring creative possibilities, expanding the horizons of human creativity.

The MIT Media Lab exemplifies a successful environment that fosters creativity and innovation. This interdisciplinary research laboratory encourages collaboration among artists, engineers, and scientists to explore new ideas and technologies. With its emphasis on experimentation and hands-on learning, the Media Lab has produced groundbreaking innovations, such as wearable technology, interactive art installations, and new forms of media. By breaking down traditional disciplinary boundaries and promoting a culture of creativity, the Media Lab serves as a model for how institutions can drive innovation and problem-solving in a rational society.

• Preserve Diverse Cultural Heritage

Rationalism doesn't seek to erase cultural identity but to preserve and celebrate it in a thoughtful and respectful way. It involves understanding the value of different cultural practices and traditions without blindly accepting the irrational aspects often embedded in them. A rational society appreciates cultural diversity as a product of human creativity and history, using it to build connections across communities. For instance, rationalism supports preserving languages, art forms, and historical landmarks, while encouraging dialogue that questions practices rooted in superstition or exclusion. Rational preservation of culture promotes both diversity and progress, fostering an inclusive society.

Schools and community organizations can implement programs that explore local traditions, languages, and customs, fostering appreciation for cultural diversity. For example, the "Cultural Heritage Education" program in Scotland engages students in learning about their heritage through hands-on activities, storytelling, and community involvement. This approach not only instills a sense of pride in one's own culture but also cultivates empathy and respect for others.

In an age where cultural practices may be at risk of disappearing, documenting and digitizing cultural heritage is crucial. This includes recording oral histories, traditional practices, and local languages. Projects like the "Endangered Languages Project" aim to document and preserve languages at risk of extinction through audio recordings and digital archives. By utilizing technology to capture and share cultural heritage, we ensure that future generations can access and learn from these valuable resources, fostering a greater understanding of cultural diversity.

Cultural festivals and events play a significant role in preserving and promoting diverse cultural heritage. These gatherings provide opportunities for individuals to share their traditions, music, dance, and cuisine, fostering community engagement and cultural exchange. For instance, the "Festival of Nations" in the United States celebrates the rich cultural diversity of the country, showcasing performances, food, and crafts from various ethnic groups. Such events promote cross-cultural understanding and appreciation while reinforcing the importance of preserving diverse heritage.

Supporting indigenous communities in preserving their languages, traditions, and practices is essential for maintaining cultural richness. Initiatives like the "First Peoples' Cultural Council" in Canada focus on revitalizing Indigenous languages and arts through funding, training, and community engagement. By empowering Indigenous voices and supporting their cultural practices, societies can recognize and honor the value of diverse cultural heritage.

Implementing laws that protect cultural sites, artifacts, and practices is essential for safeguarding heritage. For example, UNESCO's "World Heritage Convention" aims to protect cultural and natural heritage around the world by designating sites of outstanding universal value. Advocating for policies that prioritize cultural preservation ensures that heritage is recognized as a fundamental aspect of societal identity and collective memory.

Programs that facilitate cross-cultural interactions, such as artist residencies, cultural exchanges, and collaborative projects, allow individuals to learn from one another and appreciate diverse perspectives. For example, the "Sister Cities International" program connects cities across the globe to promote cultural understanding and collaboration through shared projects and exchanges. Such initiatives strengthen ties between communities, fostering a sense of global citizenship and appreciation for cultural diversity.

The Smithsonian Institution in the United States exemplifies a commitment to preserving diverse cultural heritage. With its numerous museums and research centers, the Smithsonian collects, preserves, and shares artifacts and knowledge from various cultures, emphasizing the importance of diversity in the American experience. Programs like the "Smithsonian Folklife Festival" celebrate cultural traditions through performances, workshops, and discussions, showcasing the richness of diverse heritages. By promoting cultural heritage in an engaging and educational manner, the Smithsonian helps foster appreciation for diversity while contributing to a rational understanding of cultural histories.

- Mental and Physical Health Awareness

A society grounded in rationality must prioritize both mental and physical health. Rational decision-making in these areas helps individuals make informed choices about their well-being. Mental health awareness is crucial for breaking down stigmas and addressing issues like stress, anxiety, and depression through evidence-based treatments. Similarly, rational thinking encourages physical health through practices like exercise, balanced diets, and preventive care. By promoting awareness of the benefits of maintaining health, society can reduce healthcare costs, increase productivity, and improve overall quality of life. A rational approach to health recognizes the interconnectedness of body and mind, leading to more holistic well-being.

Education systems must incorporate comprehensive health education that covers both mental and physical health topics. This education should go beyond basic information and include practical skills for managing stress, recognizing mental health issues, and understanding the importance of physical fitness. Some schools in Finland have integrated well-being education into their curricula, teaching students about nutrition, exercise, mindfulness, and emotional regulation. By equipping young individuals with knowledge and skills related to health, we empower them to make informed decisions throughout their lives.

One of the major barriers to addressing mental health is the stigma that surrounds it. To promote mental health awareness, it is essential to foster open discussions about mental health challenges and encourage individuals to seek help when needed. Campaigns like the "Time to Change" initiative in the UK aim to reduce stigma by sharing personal stories and providing resources for mental health support. By normalizing conversations about mental health, we create an environment where individuals feel safe to discuss their struggles and seek assistance, leading to a more supportive and understanding society.

We need to ensure access to mental health services, this includes not only therapy and counseling services but also preventative care and community support programs. Governments and organizations should work to expand access to mental health resources, particularly in underserved areas. The "Mental Health First Aid" program trains individuals to recognize and respond to mental health crises, helping bridge the gap between those in need and available resources. By prioritizing mental health care accessibility, societies can better support individuals facing mental health challenges.

Communities should encourage active lifestyles through various initiatives, such as creating safe public spaces for exercise, offering fitness programs, and promoting active transportation (walking, biking, etc.). Cities like Copenhagen have invested in cycling infrastructure, leading to increased physical activity among residents. By prioritizing physical fitness and providing opportunities for exercise, societies can improve public health and reduce the incidence of lifestyle-related diseases.

Mindfulness practices and stress reduction techniques into daily life can significantly impact mental health. Schools, workplaces, and community organizations can offer programs that teach mindfulness, meditation, and relaxation techniques. For example, the "Mindfulness in Schools" project teaches mindfulness techniques to students, helping them manage stress and improve focus. By promoting mindfulness practices, we empower individuals to better cope with stressors, enhancing their overall mental well-being.

Healthcare systems should encourage collaboration between physical and mental health practitioners to provide comprehensive care. Integrative health clinics that offer both medical and mental health services can address the whole person rather than treating symptoms in isolation. This approach fosters a more complete understanding of health, enabling individuals to make informed decisions about their well-being.

The World Health Organization (WHO) has launched a Mental Health Action Plan aimed at promoting mental health awareness globally. This initiative focuses on improving mental health services, reducing stigma, and integrating mental health into primary healthcare systems. By emphasizing the importance of mental health as part of overall health, the WHO encourages countries to adopt comprehensive strategies that address mental health challenges while promoting awareness and understanding.

• Time and Money Management Skill Development

Effective time and money management are essential components of a rational lifestyle. Rational decision-making includes managing personal resources efficiently to achieve long-term success and fulfillment. Teaching individuals how to prioritize tasks, set goals, and manage their finances ensures a more productive society. For instance, rational budgeting and saving strategies help people avoid debt, plan for the future, and make informed investments. Time management skills foster better work-life balance and increased efficiency in both personal and professional settings. A rational society values these skills as they contribute to personal and collective growth.

The "Jump$tart Coalition for Personal Financial Literacy" in the United States provides resources and guidelines for teaching financial literacy at various education levels. By instilling financial literacy from a young age, we equip individuals with the knowledge needed to make rational financial decisions throughout their lives.

Communities and organizations can offer workshops and seminars focused on time and money management skills. These workshops can cover various topics, including setting financial goals, creating budgets, managing debt, and maximizing productivity. Nonprofit organizations like "Operation HOPE" provide financial education workshops to underserved communities, helping individuals improve their financial skills and access economic opportunities. By providing practical knowledge and tools, these initiatives empower individuals to take charge of their financial futures.

Encouraging the use of budgeting apps, financial planning software, and productivity tools can help individuals track their expenses, set goals, and prioritize tasks. Apps like "Mint" allow users to connect their bank accounts, track spending, and create budgets in real time. By promoting technology that facilitates effective time and money management, societies can empower individuals to make informed decisions based on data rather than impulsive actions.

Encouraging individuals to prioritize work-life balance is essential for effective time management. Organizations can implement policies that promote flexible work schedules, encourage breaks, and prioritize employee well-being. For example, companies like Google have adopted flexible work hours and provide spaces for relaxation and creativity. By emphasizing work-life balance, we allow individuals to manage their time more effectively, reducing stress and enhancing productivity.

The National Endowment for Financial Education (NEFE) is a nonprofit organization in the United States dedicated to improving financial literacy and providing resources for effective money management. NEFE's "High School Financial Planning Program" offers free educational resources for educators to teach students essential financial skills. This initiative has positively impacted thousands of students by providing them with the tools needed to make informed financial decisions.

- Normalize Educational Qualification in Politics

A rational society requires leaders who possess not only political acumen but also solid educational backgrounds. Decisions made by politicians affect millions of people, and those decisions should be informed by critical thinking, evidence-based analysis, and an understanding of complex issues. Normalizing educational qualifications for political candidates ensures that leaders are equipped with the knowledge to make rational, well-informed decisions. A leader with an educational background in economics, science, or social policy, for example, will be better suited to address issues like climate change, economic inequality, and healthcare reform. Rational governance demands leaders who prioritize the common good, grounded in rational thought and scientific principles.

Countries like Australia and Canada have taken steps in this direction by requiring specific educational credentials for public office holders. For instance, in Australia, the "Parliamentary Qualifications Act" outlines certain criteria that candidates must meet. By setting minimum educational standards, we encourage a political landscape where informed individuals can participate, reducing the risk of electing leaders lacking the necessary knowledge to make sound decisions.

By offering courses and workshops on governance, public policy, and critical thinking, they can equip individuals with the knowledge necessary to engage in political discourse. Programs like "The Center for Civic Education" in the United States provide resources to educators, enabling them to teach students about the importance of political participation and the roles of government. By fostering a politically educated populace, we create a foundation for rational decision-making in politics.

Investing in leadership development initiatives that focus on nurturing the next generation of political leaders is crucial. These programs can provide aspiring politicians with training in critical thinking, ethics, public speaking, and policy analysis. For instance, organizations like "The Leadership Conference on Civil and Human Rights" in the U.S. focus on developing leaders who can navigate complex social issues effectively. By providing mentorship and training opportunities, we empower future leaders to approach political challenges with a rational mindset.

In the United Kingdom, the "Parliamentary Standards Authority" oversees the conduct of Members of Parliament (MPs) and sets standards for their qualifications. While there are no formal educational requirements to become an MP, there are ongoing discussions about establishing minimum educational standards to enhance the professionalism and accountability of elected officials. This initiative reflects a growing recognition of the need for educated leaders in governance.

CHAPTER XXII

Rationalists vs. Atheists

In contemporary discourse, the terms "rationalist" and "atheist" are often conflated, leading many to mistakenly assume that they represent the same worldview. However, a crucial distinction exists between these two philosophies that merits exploration and clarification.

To understand the differences, let's first look at the definitions of atheism. According to the Oxford Dictionary, an atheist is defined as "a person who disbelieves or lacks belief in the existence of God or gods." The Cambridge Dictionary elaborates that an atheist is "someone who does not believe in any god or gods, or who believes that no god or gods exist." The Encyclopaedia Britannica describes atheism as "the critique and denial of metaphysical beliefs in God or spiritual beings."

When we analyze these definitions, it's evident that atheism is fundamentally a belief system. Atheists operate from the standpoint that there is no God, which is a belief in itself. This belief system can often lead to a closed-minded stance where alternative possibilities, including the existence of a deity, are not considered.

In contrast, rationalism is characterized by an unwavering commitment to evaluation and openness. A rationalist does not adhere to fixed beliefs; instead, they base their understanding on evidence and logical reasoning. From a rationalist perspective, the stance regarding the existence of God might be articulated as follows: "I do not currently find any valid proof for the existence of God; however, if presented with logical evidence, I am open to reevaluation." This open-ended approach is foundational to rationalism.

While an atheist holds a firm belief in the non-existence of God, a rationalist maintains a critical distance from all beliefs, including atheism itself. Therefore, a rationalist will not reject the idea of God outright; rather, they will assess the evidence (or lack thereof) surrounding such claims. This fundamental openness to new information and willingness to adapt one's beliefs based on rational evaluation is what separates rationalists from atheists.

The essence of rationalism lies in its rejection of dogma. Individuals driven by a belief—whether it is theism, atheism, or any other ideology—are not engaging in rational thought when they refuse to evaluate contrary evidence. This indicates that a belief in non-existence, such as that held by atheists, similarly places them outside the rationalist framework. Both atheists and theists can become defensive about their respective positions, much like a person who identifies with any rigid ideological stance, such as communism or other political doctrines.

While atheism and rationalism may appear similar on the surface due to their shared critique of religious dogma, they represent fundamentally different approaches to understanding the world. Atheists hold a specific belief about the non-existence of deities, while rationalists prioritize evidence and remain open to new ideas and perspectives. Recognizing this distinction is vital for fostering meaningful discussions about belief, knowledge, and understanding in our increasingly complex world.

CHAPTER XXIII

Let the World Unite

The formation of an organized rational society is not merely an option; it is an absolute necessity for the advancement of humanity. Without a cohesive framework that promotes rational thought, faith-based ideologies will continue to evolve and adapt to contemporary challenges, finding new and insidious ways to limit human potential. Even if just one individual fails to harness their full rational capabilities, it represents a significant loss—not only for that person but for humanity as a whole. It compromises countless possibilities for progress and understanding. A rational society is essential to ensure that conservative dogma does not establish an unassailable stronghold over our collective psyche.

Some may argue that if an individual finds happiness in their own realm of faith and does not harm others, there is no reason to intervene. While this perspective seems benign on the surface, a closer examination reveals its broader implications. Personal beliefs and practices do not exist in a vacuum; they inevitably influence others. For example, when a person engages in unscientific religious rituals within their home, their children observe and internalize these behaviors. These children may later discuss their unscientific beliefs in school or other social settings, perpetuating a cycle of misinformation. Over time, they may develop the mindset that a higher power governs human lives, diminishing their sense of agency and responsibility for their actions. This limited worldview can hinder their performance in various aspects of life—be it in the workplace, personal relationships, or community involvement. Furthermore, these beliefs can spread outward, affecting colleagues, friends, and extended family, thereby amplifying their impact on society.

This phenomenon is particularly pronounced in today's world, especially in countries like India, where political parties often intertwine their platforms with religious ideologies. Such faith-based perspectives frequently undermine principles of equality and rational discourse. The self-protective mechanisms we discussed earlier in this book serve to reinforce this cycle, creating an environment where dogma thrives at the expense of reason.

Culturally, society teaches us not to challenge or "hurt" anyone's religious beliefs. But if it is deemed unacceptable to offend faith-based ideologies, then why should it be acceptable to undermine rational thought? The rationalist mindset faces daily assaults—from wasteful religious practices in temples to the pollution of sacred rivers for rituals. If religion has established norms to protect its beliefs, it stands to reason that a similar framework should be created to defend rationalism.

It is crucial to remember that knowledge is the highest form of devotion. To approach truth, one must observe, evaluate, and understand. There is no viable path to truth that bypasses the essential process of knowledge acquisition through these steps.

In the pursuit of establishing a rational society, we must be prepared for backlash. The defensive mechanisms of faith will likely respond vigorously to any perceived threat. We must remain steadfast in our commitment to rationalism, understanding that such resistance is a natural part of the process. By uniting under the banner of reason, we can collectively challenge irrationality, foster meaningful dialogue, and pave the way for a more enlightened and equitable world.

Epilogue

As we conclude this exploration of rationalism and its vital role in shaping a more enlightened society, it is essential to reflect on the journey we have undertaken. This book has delved into the intricacies of rational thought, emphasizing the necessity of nurturing a mindset rooted in logic, critical thinking, and empirical evidence. We have examined the profound impact that education, culture, and social structures have on the development of rationality, and we have outlined strategies for fostering a rational society that can resist the encroachments of dogma and superstition.

The world stands at a crossroads, where the choices we make today will determine the trajectory of future generations. In a time when misinformation and irrational beliefs threaten to undermine our collective progress, the call for a rational society has never been more urgent. As individuals, we hold the power to influence our communities, challenge established norms, and advocate for a world built on reason and understanding.

Our commitment to rationalism must extend beyond the pages of this book. It requires active participation in dialogues that promote reason, the dissemination of knowledge that encourages critical thinking, and the cultivation of environments where questioning is welcomed rather than stifled. Together, we can create a ripple effect that transforms our societies, fostering an ethos where rational inquiry flourishes.

Pledge

""I pledge to embrace rational inquiry, committing myself to question beliefs, challenge assumptions, and seek evidence in all areas of my life. I recognize that the pursuit of knowledge is a lifelong journey and will embrace curiosity as my guiding principle. I will promote education and critical thinking, advocating for educational systems that prioritize creativity and the understanding of rational principles, while supporting initiatives that encourage dialogue and the examination of diverse perspectives. I vow to empower others—especially women and marginalized groups—by sharing knowledge, fostering rational thinking, and creating supportive environments that encourage open discussions about beliefs and ideas. I will champion environmental and social responsibility, remaining aware of my impact on the world and making informed decisions that promote sustainability, equality, and human welfare. I will stand united against dogma, confronting irrational beliefs and practices with respect and compassion, knowing that change often requires patience, and engaging in constructive dialogues. Lastly, I will celebrate cultural diversity, honoring and preserving diverse heritages while ensuring that these traditions do not obstruct rational discourse. In taking this pledge, I commit myself to the creation of a society that values reason, fosters knowledge, and embraces the rich tapestry of human experience. Together, we

can forge a brighter future—one illuminated by the light of rational thought, compassion, and shared understanding."